KAIJA

SAARIAHO

WOMEN COMPOSERS

The short, readable books in the Women Composers series will introduce significant women composers to students and general readers and provide a convenient reference for performers and scholars.

Series books will treat the broadest range of women composers, combining concise biographical information with a comprehensive survey of works.

A list of books in the series appears at the end of this book.

Kaija Saariaho

Pirkko Moisala

UNIVERSITY OF ILLINOIS PRESS
Urbana and Chicago

Manufactured
in the United States
of America
C 5 4 3 2 1
This book is printed
on acid-free paper.

Library of Congress Cataloging-in-Publication Data
Moisala, Pirkko.
Kaija Saariaho / Pirkko Moisala.
p. cm. — (Women composers)
Includes bibliographical references and index.
ISBN 978-0-252-03277-6 (cloth : alk. paper)
1. Saariaho, Kaija—Criticism and interpretation.
2. Music—20th century—History and criticism.
3. Music—21st century—History and criticism.
I. Title.
ML410.S114M65 2009
780.92—dc22 [B] 2008037211

CONTENTS

PREFACE vii

1. Biography *1*
2. Developments *26*
3. Work *52*
4. Sounds *73*
5. Dramas *93*

NOTES 109

SELECTED WORKS 120

SELECTED LISTENING 121

FOR FURTHER READING 123

INDEX 125

PREFACE

THIS BOOK ON KAIJA SAARIAHO—her career, reception, composition process, musical thinking, and development as a composer—was written out of love for her music. Particularly since the successful European and U.S. premiers of her first opera, *L'amour de loin*, in 2000 and 2001, Saariaho's music has been played frequently and praised widely in the international arenas of Western art music. While I was finalizing the manuscript, in November 2007, Saariaho was chosen by Musical America as the composer of the year. As a whole, her career provides an illuminating example of the work and working contexts of a successful contemporary composer—who just happens to be a woman. As a woman composer, she is the first to enter the top echelons of western art music.

By exploring the contexts of Saariaho's studies and work, her approaches to music and composition process, and her works, this book aims to identify the fundamental ingredients of her music—its central elements and aesthetics—as well as to provide insights into how it has come to be such as it is and how it has developed. When searching for the answers, I have listened to her music, studied both the scores and reviews of her works, and read her interviews in the media. In addition, I have approached Saariaho's music by using ethnographic fieldwork methods: I have interviewed Saariaho on numerous occasions; the musicians, agents, and conductors with whom she has worked, as well as other musicians and conductors familiar with her music, have also provided time for research interviews. I have also observed rehearsals and performances of her works. This kind of approach is—in the spirit of Mikhail Bakhtin—interested in the heterophony of meanings given to musical works.

I am deeply grateful for the time and attention Saariaho has given to this project; she read the manuscript twice, thus providing me with her views on the final product. I also wish to thank warmly all the other people I have interviewed during the research, particularly Anssi Karttunen, Camilla Hoitenga, Peter Sellars, Susanna Mälkki, Dawn Upshaw, Esa-Pekka Salonen, Jussi Liimatainen, Ana Murto, Kathy Nellens, and Anne Eirola. It has been a privilege to spend hundreds of hours listening to Saariaho's music in live performances, both at home and abroad, as well as in recorded form. I have also had access to Saariaho's home archives, which include compositional sketches, written scores, and reviews of her works. In addition, I utilized Finnish music archives (the Sibeliusmuseum, the National Library, and the Finnish Music Information Center). Saariaho's publisher, Chester Music, kindly provided numerous scores, promotional recordings, and critiques of her works. I am also grateful for the help I received from Lydia Kokkola, Jean-Baptiste Barrière, Judith McCulloh, Laurie Matheson, and Lea Suomela, and I gratefully wish to acknowledge the discussions I had with Anne Sivuoja-Gunaratnam during the course of four years, from 1998 to 2002, when we were planning to conduct research on Saariaho's music together.

As an internationally recognized composer, Saariaho has been interviewed hundreds of times by journalists, critics, and scholars from various countries. Often these interviews, including my own, address similar aspects of her career and music, merely expressing the same issues slightly differently. I have provided references to published interviews only in case of direct quotations or if the same information is not included in my own interviews.

Finally, writing this book would not have been possible without the invaluable financial support from the Finland's Academy, the Jenny and Antti Wihuri Foundation, and the Foundation of the Åbo Akademi University.

KAIJA

SAARIAHO

I Biography

KAIJA SAARIAHO (née Laakkonen) is the eldest of three children of entrepreneur Launo Laakkonen and his wife Tuovi Laakkonen. Her father's family comes from Karelia, which in nationalistic discourses has been referred to as the mythical home of original Finnish culture. In the peace treaties after the Second World War, Finland was forced to cede parts of Karelia, the easternmost part of the country, to the Soviet Union. Approximately half a million people were evacuated to other areas of Finland. The Laakkonen family was one of those forced to flee from Karelia at that time. They moved to Helsinki, where Launo Laakkonen, who today is an inventor holding several patents, established a modest enterprise.

As a child, Kaija Laakkonen spent much time alone, partly due to her poor health. She remembers being an overly sensitive child who was fascinated by all kinds of sounds. Her earliest childhood memories are of being ill and looking out at other children playing outside. "I loved the quietness of the house, and I can still feel the warm touch of the spring sun on my skin. I placed a towel on a sunny spot on the floor and I lay down on it, changing my position according to the sun and enjoying the feel of the sun on my skin. That experience of sunlight and its warmth is fundamental to me."[1]

As a child, Kaija often listened to Bach's music; she thought "Bach" (German for stream) was the perfect name for this music. She also heard music from within herself. Once she asked her mother where the sounds and music she heard beneath her pillow came from. Only years later did she understand that the music she was referring to was a product of her imagination, and that other people's imaginations did not necessarily work in the same way.

Kaija's childhood summers were filled with the feeling of freedom. She spent them in her mother's childhood village, Särkisalmi, in eastern Finland (Photo 1). The children played freely in the fields and in the forests. Kaija Saariaho remembers the birds filling the air with their songs particularly vividly, and since then, the birds have felt important to her; "my favorite activity was to walk in the forest after the rain, when the leaves of the trees were still wet. They reflected the bird song differently—the forest was like a great echoing hall."[2] Kaija Saariaho's lonely childhood years have remained with her to this day.

Kaija's parents placed her in the Helsinki Rudolf Steiner School, which is equivalent to the Waldorf School in the United States.[3] The school's educational system is based on the pedagogy of German philosopher Rudolf Steiner (1861–1925), which regards the person as a bodily, mental, and spiritual being. It aims at strengthening the individuality of the pupil and broadening her or his personality.

Photo 1: On the grandmother's lap (1954). Photo: Launo Laakkonen, by permission of Kaija Saariaho.

The arts are regarded as important pedagogical means in this personal development. One of the main principles of Steiner pedagogy is that the child has to experience the concepts and forms before she or he can understand them; the experience helps the child to internalize the movement of the form. Forms are exercised by dancing, drawing, and so on. Form drawing and eurhythmy, or dance therapy, are also Steinerian pedagogical methods. Form drawing, which is part of the school curriculum during the five first years, includes exercises in symmetrical and mirror forms. The children are also asked to draw metamorphoses of a form: in the course of the exercise a simple form is transformed into another form. Kaija spent all thirteen of her school years in this school system (Photo 2). She can still recall her first school days. "When I think about the form drawings of my early school years, I remember the symmetrical exercises with the right and left hands and the satisfaction which I gained from those exercises. I am left-handed, and I felt physical uncertainty about having to act in a world where most people grasped with a different hand from me. Form drawing calmed me in this respect."[4]

Encouraged by the school's music teacher, Kaija's parents paid for her to take lessons. At first, Kaija played the violin. "The violin was my first instrument and I liked it a lot. But the gap between my own playing and the violin of my dreams was huge, too big. I wanted to try the piano. At the age of eight, I wrote in my diary that, when I returned from a skiing holiday, I found a piano waiting for me in the living room and I was about to fall on my back for pure happiness!"[5] Later, the guitar took the place of the violin. She made several secret attempts at writing music on paper at the age of ten. However, to her confusion, she could only

Photo 2: The graduation fest of the Helsinki Rudolf Steiner School (Helsinki, 1972). Photo: Launo Laakkonen, by permission of Kaija Saariaho.

write "nervous, yellow music," the echoes of which haunted her. She compared her modest compositions with those of Mozart, who had composed symphonies at the age of eleven, and this discouraged her from even dreaming about a career as a composer.

During her first years of music lessons, Kaija was taught by private teachers. Later, she continued her music studies at a music school. Education in Finnish music schools is structured around yearly graded performances. Kaija did not feel at home in this system. She loved playing, but disliked performing to an audience. Compulsory exams made her unhappy because she felt that, as a performer, she could not do justice to the music. She felt so nervous that her hands refused to obey her. The discouraging example of Mozart did not hinder Kaija from beginning to practice composing regularly from the age of seventeen on.

When Kaija was fifteen, her father's enterprise, which produced public shelters, began to expand into the successful factory it is today. Launo and Tuovi Laakkonen were not particularly interested in music; they favored the visual arts. Today, Launo Laakkonen's private collections of art range from the works of Finnish masters to works by international modernists. The visual arts were also of great interest to the young Kaija, whose favorite hobby, after music, was drawing.

After her graduation from Helsinki Rudolf Steiner School in 1972, Kaija was admitted to the Institute of Industrial Arts and Crafts,[6] where she concentrated on learning graphics. At the same time, she continued to study music at the Helsinki Conservatory (1972–76), where she took piano and organ lessons and completed the required courses in music theory and history. During this period, she also took courses in musicology, art history, and literature at Helsinki University. Experimenting with a range of topics before selecting an area of specialization was a common practice among Finnish students at that time.

Although Kaija studied the visual arts, she knew that she preferred to study composition. She did not believe she could become a composer, because her ideas about creativity and what composers were like did not match her sense of self. Her image of what composers were like was largely inspired by Beethoven and Jean Sibelius, the Finnish national hero who was always pictured as a sturdy old man with a big cigar.[7] For Kaija, at that time, a real composer was a decidedly serious, male character: "It was totally unlike my own image [of a composer], both externally and internally. The things you read about great composers as a child—and, in addition, the image one has about Sibelius. These were the thoughts which paralyzed me, because I did not imagine fulfilling these images." The curriculum of music history and the standard repertoire of concerts did not include women composers, not even Clara Schumann or Barbara Strozzi. Ida Moberg

(1859–1947), the first woman composer in Finland, was completely forgotten. Kaija felt that "composing and music were such great things that a simple girl like myself could not manage them."

During her early student years, Kaija was briefly married to Markku Saariaho, whose surname she still uses. After her divorce, she lived with a painter, Olli Lyytikäinen (1949–87). During the seven years (1972–79) they lived together, Lyytikäinen produced dozens of paintings of his partner. Their home in central Helsinki was the venue for evening gatherings of artists, musicians, and composers.

Saariaho's need to compose became so urgent that, in 1976, she wished to enroll as a composition student at the foremost school of music in the country, the Sibelius Academy. She insisted that the composition teacher, Paavo Heininen (b. 1938), accept her as a student. The way Saariaho describes her internal calling corresponds closely to the romantic idea of an artist who is driven by the compulsory need to create. "The only thing that meant anything to me was music, and not being able to make it was unbearable. It was an internal need to become a composer. Music and I, we belonged together."

Thanks to Sibelius, the status of composers has always been exceptionally high in Finland. As a small (5 million inhabitants) and relatively young (independent since 1917) country, Finland has needed—and still needs—international success stories in different streams of life: in sports, in economics, and in the arts and music. Athletes and artists, musicians and composers, who have claimed international success often become national heroes. However, the route to becoming an international artist has been different for Finnish women in comparison to that of their male counterparts. Saariaho also had to struggle to make her way as a composer.

Heininen, who had studied under the guidance of Bernd Alois Zimmermann (1918–70) and Vincent Persichetti (1915–87), accepted Saariaho into his composition class of 1976 even though it was already full. Saariaho left her studies in graphics and musicology and dedicated herself to composition. As a composer, Heininen was, as a post-serialist, one of the few refreshing exceptions in the mainstream of nationalistic relativism in Finland in the 1960s and 1970s. He had developed his own method of teaching composition, the kernel of which was atonal contrapuntal writing.

The Finnish music culture of the 1970s did not encourage Saariaho to study composition. Saariaho found her role models in the other arts: the authors Virginia Woolf and Anaïs Nin, and the poets Sylvia Plath and Edith Södergran. The third symphony of the only recognized Finnish woman composer of the time, Helvi Leiviskä (1902–82), was premiered in 1976. Saariaho could not regard Leiviskä as a role model; she was not inspired by her neo-romantic works. Without precursors, it was hard for Saariaho to feel validated as a composer. The differences between the image she had of a composer and her self-image created an internal conflict, "an anxiety of authorship,"[8] which she initially tried to overcome by attempting to mask her femininity. "At some point of time [at the age of around twenty], I began to smoke cigars and tried to give a stronger impression of myself. However, that passed by quickly. Since then, I haven't had such problems with my self-image."

The contradiction between Saariaho's image of a composer and her image of herself may have been a central factor in "paralyzing" her creativity. Heininen was a demanding, severe teacher who forced her to become more confident. Among other things, he insisted that she look at the mirror twenty times a day and say, "I can!" "I was terribly insecure, after all, at that time in my life and also in my composing work. It had something to do with my identity as a young woman. I felt that Paavo pulled me back to life." Heininen encouraged each student to find his or her own musical language. With his support, Saariaho rediscovered the creativity she had experienced as a child: "all those colors, seeing, hearing, and living in the intermingling dimensions of all the senses, zooming in and out, making great, free associations; I had been there before." Once again, she experienced music free from the anxieties she had felt as a performing musician.

Saariaho studied with Heininen for four years; his guidance was crucial for her early development as a composer. At first, she could only compose songs and other vocal music inspired by literature and poems, but her teacher insisted that she begin to write for instruments. Saariaho discovered that the strings and the flute fed her musical ideas best. As time passed, she found a similar way of writing for the voice as well.

In the 1960s, the state of Finland had established a network of music schools, which provided solid education for musically talented youth. The results of this education, the highly trained student community working at the Sibelius Academy, provided a fruitful foundation for Saariaho's early development as a composer. The same generation of students included the composer Magnus Lindberg (b. 1958), who also studied composition under Heininen, along with the conductors Jukka-Pekka Saraste (b. 1956) and Esa-Pekka Salonen (b. 1958). Salonen recalls how he "could immediately sense that Kaija [was] a highly original, creative person with a strong will although she was a bit shy about her musicianship, which, at that point in time, was perhaps not as strong as the instrumental background the rest of us had. Other composers, such as Berlioz and Wagner, have also come from such backgrounds."[9]

Together with these and other fellow students, Saariaho established an association called Korvat auki! (Ears Open!), the aim of which was to counteract the conservative nationalistic tropes of Finnish art music. Ears Open!, which in addition to composers also engaged conductors, musicians, and musicologists, turned to Central European avant-garde for inspiration. When the Sibelius Academy refused the students' request for a course on the analysis of contemporary music, they began to hold study group meetings in their homes. Each student took a turn presenting an analysis of some contemporary work to the group for discussion. Saariaho remembers how ambitious these meetings were; "we had naturally to show to the others how smart and innovative we were."[10] Ears Open! also promoted contemporary music with concerts given in the countryside, suburban areas, and schools. Ears Open! was born, of course, as a reaction of very young people to their surroundings and time. Salonen describes the basic ideas of these activities with nostalgic irony: "We thought that the people needed post-serial music and they had been neglected for a long time in Finland where post-serial music had been enjoyed only by privileged; our idea was to bring it to all people."[11]

There was no particular aesthetic proclamation in Ears Open! ; according to Salonen, it merely defined "what music should not be: music may not be tonal, music may not be modal, music may not be easily understandable—the form of music must be complex."[12] Saariaho, who was the president of the association in 1979–80, remembers that "it felt as if we did not have place in that culture and that we had plenty of things to do which no-one else did. We were upset that most of the financial support went to the operas of Joonas Kokkonen and Aulis Sallinen."[13]

The activity of the young music students later led to the establishment of the Avanti! chamber orchestra, which also played an important role in promoting contemporary music; "it was important to the composers that there were musicians who wanted to play contemporary music and who played it well—everything grew within the same family, composers, conductors, and musicians, and even though these professions grew later on apart, the same natural way of interacting continued."[14]

Collaboration between the founding members of Ears Open! continues today in several ways. One fruit of this early collaboration, Summer Sounds, a music festival born around Avanti! and held in Porvoo, a town near Helsinki, gathers old friends together each summer.[15] Collaboration between Saariaho and Esa-Pekka Salonen, who has worked as the principal conductor of the Los Angeles Philharmonic since 1992, has produced both premiers of Saariaho's works conducted by Salonen, as well as CD-recordings of her music (see Selected Listening). One of the founding members of Ears Open!, Jussi Liimatainen, currently a professor of sound technology, worked as a sound technician for many of Saariaho's electronic works and their live electronic performances.

Saariaho's original interest in electronic music grew out of dissatisfaction with the acoustics of the concert places where contemporary music was performed in Helsinki. Within Finnish art music circles, electronics were not readily accepted. The media reception of electronic works was mainly negative when Saariaho's first tape work, *Cartolina per Siena* (1979), was performed. She composed this work after Franco Donatoni's (1927–2000) summer course in Siena, Italy, in the composition workshop of the Young Nordic Music Festival in Arvika, Sweden. Even though there was an electronic music studio in the Department of Musicology at Helsinki University, the electronic equipment of the Swedish studio was much more developed. The use of electronics was still subject to prejudice in the early 1980s; the music critic Seppo Heikinheimo from the main Finnish newspaper wrote, "only the weakest composers need support of 'computer crutches'; they are more interested in bustling with numbers and buttons than scratching slowly dazzling visions of sound on paper."[16]

Much to Saariaho's annoyance, the media drew attention to her gender and her use of computers. As a woman composer composing electronic music, Saariaho had to struggle against two kinds of prejudices; "who would listen to Saariaho's music if she were an ugly woman,"[17] wrote Heikinheimo in a column where he discussed the influence of composers' and musicians' looks on the perception of music. The combination, a woman composing with the help of computers, was regarded as an astonishing, exotic oddity. However, Saariaho's use of computers reduced the extent to which her works were regarded as feminine.

The supportive circle of friends and multifaceted opportunities open to the composition students eased Saariaho's path. Festivals for young Nordic composers provided important venues where ideas and influences could be exchanged across borders. Since the early years of the nation, sending talented young composers abroad to develop their musical skills and establish their identity has been customary in Finland. Young Finnish composers of Saariaho's generation had lively contacts with the broader international music field as well: they could take part in international summer courses, and they had opportunities to work in the electronic music studios abroad.

Saariaho completed her studies at the Sibelius Academy in the winter of 1980, and then the same year made her way to the summer school in Darmstadt, Germany, where spectral[18] music made by French composers Gérard Grisey (1946–98) and Tristan Murail (b. 1947) resonated well with her own musical ideas:

"I came from post-serial aesthetics, which forbid tonal explorations, and I arrived in the land of new harmonies, distantly reminiscent of music by Maurice Ravel and Claude Debussy." In Darmstadt, she met Brian Ferneyhough (b. 1943), and continued to study composition under his and Klaus Huber's (b. 1924) lead in Freiburg Musikhochschule in Germany. However, she found their strict post-serial aesthetics limiting; she was annoyed by the emphasis placed on the intellect, "as if it were more important than other experiences, expressions, and ways of life."[19] The complex techniques and inaudible structures that the other students presented did not feed Saariaho's own musical ideas. Instead of learning to structure scholarly scores, she wanted to create communicative, audible musical forms.

Saariaho received her diploma in composition from Freiburg Musikhochschule in 1983. Around the same time, Saariaho met in Darmstadt the American-born flutist, Camilla Hoitenga (b. 1954), with whom she has collaborated ever since. She showed Saariaho technicalities of playing the flute and discussed technical solutions for flute compositions. Hoitenga was deeply impressed by the originality of Saariaho's first composition for solo flute, *Laconisme de aile* (1982). It was totally unlike the controlled, precise flute works of Karl-Heinz Stockhausen (1928–2007) with which Hoitenga was more familiar.[20]

In early 1982, Saariaho also attended a major computer music course at the Institut de Recherche et Coordination Acoustique/Musique (IRCAM—Institute for Music/Acoustic Research and Coordination) in Paris. IRCAM had been initiated by President Georges Pompidou and set up by the composer Pierre Boulez (b. 1925) in the early 1970s for studies in acoustics and psycho-acoustics of musical sound employing the most up-to-date technology and computers. Saariaho began to visit Paris frequently. She was fascinated by the multiplicity of possibilities it provided; she felt that there was a place for her there.

Since 1982, Saariaho has lived and worked in Paris. She feels at home in the French culture in which the intellect and the senses do not exclude each other in everyday life. "I have an ascetic tendency of being extremely demanding toward myself, and to balance that it is good to have a lively life in my surroundings."

Saariaho's background in Finland, a state that values music and supports its composers, is reflected in her solid musical training. Another aspect of her Finnish character is her deep love of nature. In her musical production, nature—the sea, the sky, the northern lights, birds, water lilies—appears as an important inspiration for her compositions, sources of musical material as well as form-giving principles. "As a child I enjoyed walking outdoors. I loved the sounds of the forest and the birds in the summer, the light reflected by the snow, so typical of the Finnish winter, as well as the light after the darkness of polar nights. It is a part of my

Finnishness, which I still carry within me."[21] Every summer, Saariaho returns to the family's summer cottage in eastern Finland in her mother's childhood village beside Lake Simpele.

Paris and IRCAM (1982–90)

When Saariaho arrived in Paris, she hardly spoke any French, yet she had long felt a strong connection with French culture, particularly through the music of Maurice Ravel (1875–1937) and Claude Debussy (1862–1918) and works by Marcel Proust (1871–1922). The French culture was both very strange and very familiar to her. The harshness of the German culture had drawn her toward asceticism, whereas the Parisian lifestyle, with its multifaceted artistic sensations, allowed her more "space to breathe"; "it felt so good to me, the value Parisians give to their senses—the wines, the scents, the multitude of possibilities: it somehow relaxed me, gave me a freedom."[22] She also appreciated the benefits of the big multicultural city with several parallel value systems.

Paris also provided an escape from the restrictive post-serialist tradition, in which "you were not allowed to have pulse, or tonally oriented harmonies, or melodies."[23] Saariaho was tired of writing music through such negations. In Paris in the mid-1970s, the L'Itinéraire group was formed by Grisey, Murail, and a number of other composers. They followed the idea of spectral harmony, which breaks away from the equal-tempered scale. Close examinations of sound phenomena and their different parameters—pitch, duration, volume, sonority, and articulation—had played a role in European modern music since *Mode de valeurs et d'intensités* (1949) by Olivier Messiaen (1908–92). The L'Itinéraire group took the next step: it was interested in the combination of sound color and harmonics as well as in observing the capacity of human perception on all levels of the composition.[24] Their ideas developed into what is known today as spectralism, the spectral school of music. Because the compositions of spectral composers are based on the overtone spectra of sound, the resulting music sounds exotic but, at the same time, natural to the ear. The lower part of the overtone series of the spectrum (the components of sound frequencies, the hierarchy of sub-sounds, and their amplitudes) provides the fundamental pitches of Western tonal music: the octave, the fourth, the fifth, and the major third.

A single, living sound as a resonant acoustic complex became the basis for spectralism. Computational analyses of sound made calculating the combinations of the various factors of sound possible; the consonant and dissonant characteristics of different kinds of "nonmusical" sounds were also analyzed. Roughly stated, the aim of spectral composers was to make music for the ears, not for the eyes. In this way, they provided an alternative to the twelve-tone technique and serialism, which emphasized the abstract intellectualism of mathematically constructed compositions, in other words, musical structures over the sounding result. It is important to note, however, that unlike serialism and the twelve-tone technique, spectral music is not a composition technique. The studies of the acoustics and psycho-acoustics of sound also revealed information about the ear's capacity to perceive sounds and music. The composers working at IRCAM aimed at creating compositions grounded in these scientific studies of perception and experience.[25]

Murail prepared at IRCAM *Désintégrations* (1982–83) for orchestra and tape, based on an analysis of sound spectra. The basic principle of the work is the development between harmony and inharmony, which creates the impression of alternating lights and shadows.[26] *Désintégrations*, like another work produced by the early spectralist, Grisey's *Les Espaces Acoustiques*, provides glimpses of the grand, complex, and ethereal spectral harmonies. These spectralist ideas have been further developed by many composers, such as Claude Vivier and Georg Friedrich Haas as well as Saariaho. As spectralism was gaining a foothold in Europe, minimalism was developing in the North America. Even though minimalism and spectralism are very different composition styles and the resulting works cannot be compared, they both emphasize the need to return to the basics of music. This attitude provides many—both spectralist and minimalist—compositions with a kind of meditative calmness.

IRCAM's computerized and electronic facilities provided several technological novelties crucial to the development of Saariaho's musical language. She found appropriate tools for exploring the details of sound and sound processes, as well as creating new timbres and sonorities, which increased the repertoire she had already employed in Finland and Germany. She followed the example of the l'Itinérairen composers and studied different kinds of sounds in order to learn about their characteristics and to obtain material for composition. She also sought out alternative ways of organizing aspects of sound. By slowing down a sound without altering its pitch, she could examine the processes of sound in detail, as well as accentuate selected dimensions of the sound. She also performed several unfruitful experiments aimed at breaking the chromatic scale into microtonality. The analysis of the physical qualities of sound, which revealed its microtonal dimensions, finally provided her with the desired means by which she could depart from the traditional scale. She also noticed that certain playing techniques created microtonality and broke down the harmonic structure. In her experience this process was like inventing a microscope for music: "You can take one aspect of a sound that is interesting and extend that timbre through electronic processing, like the symmetrical form of a flower being dispersed by the wind."[27]

New means of synthesizing and analyzing sound made Saariaho more sensitive to the physiological bases of her musical choices and eventually enabled her to re-establish her musical language. The merciless results provided by the computer made her more aware of her musical choices, particularly of her own harmonic thinking. In a way, she used the computer as her teacher; she formalized her musical choices and generated music through the computer.

Saariaho became fascinated by hierarchies of sound color, utilizing computers to control different dimensions of music, studying the relationship between sound color and harmony, and combining acoustic instruments with electronics. The sound synthesis program *Chant*, created by Xavier Rodet and Yves Potard at IRCAM, acquainted Saariaho with the physical characteristics of sound and allowed her to create sounds similar to those of the human voice and instruments. She studied the physicality of different kinds of sounds, aiming at finding explanations for what she heard. She noticed that the more "lively" a sound is, the more it varies. For instance, in the analysis of a spoken "usshh," the richest material is at the point when *u* turns into *sh*. The most living sound is in a constant process of transmission; thus, a synthetic sound has to be varied in order to make it interesting. Saariaho also transferred this knowledge into her instrumental writing.

Saariaho collaborated with several programmers at IRCAM to develop a personal system of calculating musical structures. This system can be used to generate, in addition to pitch, other musical parameters such as dynamics, durations, motives, and timbre through interpolations (calculated transitions between two poles). The composer needs to define the total duration of the transition, as well as the beginning and ending values of the musical parameter to be interpolated. The computer program calculates the remaining values of the transition. However, Saariaho rarely accepts these mechanical calculations in her works as such: she changes the values calculated by the program later in the course of the composition process.

While working at IRCAM, Saariaho also attended the Musique Concrète Aqousmatique (musical studies of recorded concrete sounds) concerts of Radio France. She also prepared materials for the tape parts of a couple of her works, *Jardin secret II* and *Verblendungen*, in the GRM (Groupe de Recherches Musicales) studio of Radio France. It was exceptional that one and the same person worked both in IRCAM and in GRM, because these organizations represented distinctly different musical schools. GRM was the successor of Groupe de Musique Concrète, a group formed in 1951 by composers compiling compositions from concrete sounds. Musique Concrète has been traditionally opposed to electronically produced music. The GRM regarded concrete sounds as rich enough to form the material for musical works. The inspiration for this project came from Pierre Schaeffer (1910–95), who had begun to experiment with recorded natural sounds already in 1948.[28] His *Traité des objets musicaux* (1966) categorized *objèt sonore*, sound object, for instance, as transparent, soft, hard, short, and long sounds. This categorization system may have encouraged Saariaho to create her own terminology of sound dichotomies.

Musique concrète also left its marks on Saariaho's musical production, although none of her works is a pure product of this school. Somewhat typically, she adapted some of the school's ideas into her own musical thinking but did not adopt the strict rules associated with it. Two of her works, the ballet *Maa* (1991) and the radiophonic work *Stilleben* (1987–88), are closest to musique concrète, since their electronic parts mostly consist of recorded sounds in addition to other processed sounds. Saariaho usually processes recorded concrete sounds electronically instead of using them in their pure form. She may also create synthetic sounds that are like concrete or instrumental sounds. In her opinion, "the natural sounds—the wind, the sea—are the most beautiful sounds that a human being can hear; perhaps from this experience I was fascinated by producing similar kinds of sounds which, even distantly, remind me of the sounds of nature."[29]

In the early 1980s, Saariaho established a close working relationship with Anssi Karttunen (b. 1960), a Finnish-born cellist living in Paris. Together they began to look for ways to expand the sound world of the cello. They experimented with new techniques and recorded the results, which Saariaho then analyzed with the help of computer programs. Karttunen recalls that Saariaho had very precise ideas regarding the string instruments that she wanted to try out with him.[30] He introduced her to the details of various bowing techniques, which helped her to find the best ways to realize her sound ideas on a string instrument. Analyses of cello sounds increased Saariaho's sensitivity to the constant variations of the living sound. She was convinced that the sonic elements could play a role in musical structures. Today, Karttunen performs in major concert houses all over the world. Saariaho has dedicated several works to him.

Ever since these early contacts with spectral music in Paris, Saariaho has maintained her interest in sound, its dynamics, harmonic structure, and ever-changing microscopic nuances. The idea of using analyzed sound phenomena as the basis for creating harmony, initiated by the spectral composers, became central to her. The influence of musique concrète, in the form of concrete natural or electronically modified sounds such as bird songs and whispers, can also be heard in her compositions.

Saariaho decided to live in Paris, partly because it gave her the opportunity to work in electronic music studios. Her studies in France were supported for three and a half years by an artist's grant funded by the state of Finland's Committee for Music. Although Saariaho found the music laboratory of her dreams in IRCAM, its social atmosphere was overtly competitive and based on cultural models that were alien to her.[31] The center was directed by Pierre Boulez; Saariaho respected him as both a director and a composer, but she did not feel any special need to search for his advice. At IRCAM, Saariaho was the only woman composer at the time. There she obviously did not have to face prejudices against using computers in composition; however, her sex combined with new technology formed a problem: "I was often overlooked because I was a woman. If one is a woman, composer and, in addition, working with the computers, it is, for many, a shocking combination." Nevertheless, Saariaho was well aware that it was a privilege to work with the expensive computer facilities of IRCAM, unique in Europe at the time. IRCAM also provided an inspiring forum for exchanging ideas. It brought together sound technicians, composers, and scientists studying psycho-acoustics. Saariaho received the necessary technical support to enable her to realize her musical ideas.[32] During her time at IRCAM, Saariaho collaborated with the cognitive psychologist Stephen McAdams; together they studied the perception of timbre. Saariaho also wrote a couple articles on composition techniques and sound analysis.[33]

However, it was not only the resources provided by IRCAM that encouraged Saariaho to stay in Paris; during her first years in the city she got to know the composer Jean-Baptiste Barrière (b. 1958), who worked as the educational director of IRCAM (Photo 3). Today, he is regarded as one of the leading experts in computerized music and Saariaho thanks him for emotional and practical support; for instance, resonance filters used in Saariaho's compositions are developed on the basis of ideas put forward by Barrière. They were married in 1984 and lived in the tight knit community around the Pompidou center and IRCAM before moving to another location in Paris in 2005. Their children, Alexandre (b. 1989) and Aliisa (b. 1995), were born there.

Life in Paris as an unknown woman composer was not without difficulties. The living standard provided by the grant was modest, and finding a space among the French, more established composers was at times hard. These years were formational for Saariaho's identity as a foreigner living abroad in a constant state of longing, experiencing strongly the cultural borders and the difficulties of verbal communication. However, the working years at IRCAM expanded her musical vocabulary greatly. The premiere of *Verblendungen* (1982–84)—Saariaho's first major work for orchestra incorporating tape material—ended this most demanding

Photo 3. At the studio 8 of IRCAM, surrounded by computers (Paris, 1983). Photo: Jean-Baptiste Barrière.

period in her career despite the crushing reviews published by the Finnish press. According to music critic Seppo Heikinheimo from the main Finnish newspaper, Saariaho's ideas seemed "still insufficient for such large-scale works requiring a large number of performers"; he found it "boring to listen to such virtually static noise, so very boring."[34] The impression of the music critic from another Finnish newspaper had of *Verblendungen* was that it "remained flimsily slim."[35] It is, of course, impossible to know whether these negative impressions of *Verblendungen* were due to the critics' lack of familiarity with tape music or whether they were preconditioned by the composer's gender.

As a result of the hard work done in the Parisian studios, Saariaho's first international recognition came in 1986, when she was awarded the Kranichsteiner Musikpreis in Darmstadt. This marked the beginning of Saariaho's international fame. In his report, Robin Freeman described Saariaho as "very much the dedicated artist, the musician who lives for her art because nothing less will do," regarding her as "one of the most impressive presences" in Darmstadt.[36]

In the early articles, interviews, and reviews of her works published in the Finnish press, Saariaho's sex was always evoked in one way or another. In the

1980s, when feminism swept over Finnish academia and journalism, there was a social mandate for a successful woman composer; in the women's magazines, Saariaho was presented as an exceptional woman. Saariaho, however, refused to take this role; "there is no use expecting a feminist perspective from me, not to mention explaining my music as being feminine."[37] She frequently emphasized that she did not want her gender to be an issue and she did not want to be called a "woman composer" any more than she wanted to be labelled a "computer composer." She wanted people to experience her music as music instead of as music composed by a woman.

From mid-1980s on Saariaho's works were successfully performed and reviewed in Paris, London, and the major cities of the United States. She began to receive frequent commissions from concert houses, ensembles, and music festivals: *Lichtbogen* (1986) was commissioned by the French Cultural Ministry; *Io* (1987) by IRCAM; *Nymphea* (1987) for stringed quartet and live electronics by the Lincoln Center together with Doris and Myron Beigler and premiered by Kronos Quartet; and *From the Grammar of Dreams* (1988) by the Huddersfield Contemporary Music Festival. New international awards followed after only two years; *Stilleben* (1987–88), commissioned by the Finnish Broadcasting Corporation, won the Prix Italia competition in 1988 and, in the same year, she received the Danish William Hansen award and *Stilleben* and *Io* were awarded with the Golden Nica prize at the Ars Electronica Festival in Linz, Austria.

These successes guaranteed a continuation of Saariaho's artist's grant from the state of Finland, for the following five years, until 1992. The state of Finland maintains the Finnish Music Information Center (FIMIC), which supports the marketing of Finnish music by making composers and their works known and available to the public. In 1988, FIMIC published a brochure on Kaija Saariaho, in which musicologist Risto Nieminen accurately describes the two extremes of her musical path: "The road she travels connects two extreme points. At one end are form, technique, computers, systems, and rationality, at the other end dreams, timbres, moods, fragility, the senses, and intuition."[38]

The Finnish media faithfully reported the awards Saariaho received and quoted the positive reviews given by the foreign press and, when she began to gain international success, the tone of her reception gradually changed. In the beginning of the 1990s, she was no longer treated as a female curiosity among the composers in the Finnish press but, instead, as a "Finnish girl" who, in spite of her use of the latest technology still maintained the admired mythical relationship with Finnish nature. In 1991, she was one of three to receive special awards from the Finland's Cultural Foundation. Heikki Aaltoila, music critic from *Uusi Suomi*, made a revealing comment on this occasion: "The composer Kaija Saariaho, 38, who lives in Paris, works in a traditionally male field; however, the Finnish Cultural Foundation hardly gave her the prize for such a trivial reason. It is, of course, just to say that Saariaho is our most famous woman composer and the only Finnish woman composer who has gained an international reputation. Presumably, it is more correct to see her simply as a composer (sex necessary but not crucial) who has consistently proceeded along her path, avoided becoming bound by systems, by the dangers of 'brain and paper music' and created music which impresses with its human content and which is well received everywhere."[39]

In 1993, the Record of the Year, chosen by the music producers of the Finnish Broadcasting Corporation, was a recording of Saariaho's orchestral works, *Du cristal* and . . . *à la Fumée* , and the string quartet, *Nymphea* (see Selected Listening). The ultimate reward came from the Finnish state in 1994, when Saariaho received one of the five Finland Prizes for remarkable citizens.

Possibly this new atmosphere encouraged Saariaho to perform her gender differently. She gave interviews in which she commented upon her life as a mother and a composer. She also criticized the Finnish gender system. "In Finland, we have an odd situation: on the one hand, we are equal; on the other, a completely patriarchal system governs. Every area must have some kind of a father figure, Kekkonen [the former president of Finland for twenty-five years] or Kokkonen [one of the most prominent composers in Finland from the 1950s to the 1980s]—there is something inbuilt in it, the whole system of upbringing leads to that."[40] In 1991, she continued to analyze the Finnish gender structure: "All the important Finns are men, including musicians. It comes from Finnish mythology. Therefore, it is particularly difficult to become the only woman composer in Finland. There have always been Väinämöinens [the hero in Finnish national epics, *Kalevala*] who desire to rule."

International Spheres

Saariaho has been able to work as a full-time composer for most of her working career. At first, this was due to the Finnish state financial support system for composers and, since the early 1990s, to the constant flow of composition commissions from different music festivals, institutions, orchestras, and ensembles as well as the increasing number of performances of her works. The early commissions came from Finnish orchestras and European contemporary music festivals. Since her breakthrough in the mid-1980s, she has received commissions from major concert houses, orchestras, broadcasting corporations, and music festivals in Europe, Japan, and the United States. In the early 1990s, commissions were made by distinguished orchestras, such as the Los Angeles Symphony orchestra (*Du cristal*, 1989–90) and the New York Philharmonic Orchestra (*Oltra mar*, 1998–99); broadcasting corporations, such as the BBC symphony orchestra (*Graal théâtre*, 1994) and the Westdeutscher Rundfunk (*Nuits, adieux*, 1991); concert halls, such as the Barbican Center and IRCAM (*Amers*, 1992); music festivals, such as the Salzburg Music Festival (*Château de l'âme*, 1995); and the Wien Modern Festival (*Lonh*, 1996). Very few premiers of her works have taken place in her country of origin, Finland.

The 1990s was an extremely productive decade, which included several important milestones in Saariaho's career. The international scene for contemporary music is not very large; composers who make their name due to successful premiers at significant concert sites receive international recognition within these circles rather quickly. However, it is also important for contemporary composers to have their works performed on the more conservative and, simultaneously, more significant platforms for Western art music. Saariaho's career has proceeded extremely well on both fronts. Successful performances of her works have followed one another. The progress of her career is also marked by a number of awards; in 1997, she was made Chevalier de l'Ordre des Arts et Lettres, granted by the state of France; in 1999, she received the Elsie Stoeger Prize awarded by The Chamber Music Society of Lincoln Center, New York; in 2006, she was, again, honored by being made Chevalier de l'Ordre National du Mérite in France.

Saariaho worked and composed at CARL at the University of California, San Diego, in 1988–89, and more briefly at the Center for Computer Music and Music Technology in Tokyo in 1993. These visits have left their marks on her compositions; she was particularly impressed by Japanese aesthetics. In Japan, Saariaho wrote *Six Japanese Gardens* (1993/1995), in memory of Toru Takemitsu (1930–96), during the two and half months she worked in Tokyo. Before her visit, she decided to compose a work for percussion. She did not know much about Japanese culture, but she wanted to hear traditional Japanese music and theater. She was very impressed by almost everything she experienced, but especially by the gardens of Kioto. She admired the sensitivity with which the garden designers use different kinds of materials, sand, stones, and moss, and found similarities between their architectural composition and the architecture of music. "When I learned in Kyoto about the way the traditional gardens are designed, how the travelling of the eye is planned, I felt a connection between architecture and music: both art forms select and introduce materials, let them grow, give them form, prepare new contrasting elements, create different relations between the materials."[41] In the moss gardens, she experienced a special kind of atmosphere, which reminded her of the temporal essence of music; "it is about the art of time, a garden becoming the art of time."[42]

The gardens even provided some of the details of the compositions: "The idea of a stone garden is that there are clusters of stone and sand which are raked into waves. In my mind, the waves were transformed into polyrhythmic parts and the stones into the strokes of cymbals. I had tuned my mind for a composition for percussion. Then, when I was actually there, I examined the gardens through my filters of thought. That's how it often happens: I decide on the points of departure, but stay open to other aspects—I allow things to flow in and then I close the doors and begin to work."[43]

The Japanese views of time and structures fascinate Saariaho as well. She recorded the sounds of Japanese nature and traditional instruments from the large collection at the Kunitachi College of Music. She also had access to a database of recordings from which she picked, for instance, the chanting of Buddhist monks.

In certain sections of the resulting work, *Six Japanese Gardens* (1993), the musicians may sometimes choose which percussion instruments they wish to work with; Saariaho has only specified the materials—wood, stone, and metal of the instruments. The material determines the sound quality. "There are so many kinds of percussion instruments which I do not know. I thought that it would be most interesting to see how the musicians choose their instruments in certain passages."[44] The identity and character of the composition remains the same even when the instruments are changed; each musical idea requires certain kinds of sound color but not a particular instrument.

In the academic year 1997–98, Saariaho worked, together with her husband Jean-Baptiste Barrière, as a visiting professor in composition at the Sibelius Academy in Helsinki. She enjoyed her discussions with composition students and commenting upon their works, encouraging them to find their personal musical expression. However, she suffered from having too little time for composing. The family stayed in Finland for just a year, after which they returned to Paris. However, each summer, they spend time in the Laakkonen family summer cottage. Saariaho regards herself as "a Finn who is living in Paris"; she carries with her the cultural identity that was formed as a child. She finds in her own character aspects that she regards as typically Nordic, such as clearness and profoundness: "A certain healthy straightforward way of dealing with things—I like things to be clear, I like to express myself clearly—I would like to keep things simple, not complicate them. I would like to keep things profound, not superficial. These are typically Nordic features, some of the good sides of our culture."[45] Saariaho has also been asked to consider how her Finnish heritage has possibly influenced her music; "maybe one thing is this relation to the material, which is so serious and wants to be profound," she speculates.[46]

Saariaho has received all the major Finnish prizes awarded to musicians, some of them more than once. She has twice received the Janne[47] prize given by the music producers (1993 and 1997), and in 2000 her DC *From the Grammar of Dreams* was dubbed the Record of the Year. She continued to receive a state salary for composition, in 1993–2000. For the period 2005–10 she has been appointed as professor by the committee for music of the state of Finland; the professorship is a salary for composition without any other obligations. Music journalist Kai Amberla noted with pleasure how all this success has not affected Saariaho's personality: "Despite all her success Saariaho still feels shy, a bit closed, a bit uneasy about her fame. She is not a verbal master who proffers shining analyses of her works and about herself. She is, rather, an archetypal artist, who wishes to be silent and let her works speak for themselves."[48]

Even though she often has the feeling that she does not fit into any "pigeonhole" in Finnish society, Saariaho's roots and sense of belonging remain firmly in the Finnish language and nature: "the way I express myself in French is certainly very different from the way I speak in Finnish. Because, in Finnish, my use of language is so much more precise and varied—[this] gives me the feeling of being a foreigner in France."[49] Saariaho speaks Finnish with her children, who are fluent in both French and Finnish. When she is in Paris, she misses her relatives, siblings, and Finnish friends, and when she is away from Paris, she longs for her home. She is a stranger in both Finland and Paris: "When I return to Finland, everything is somehow painfully familiar, full of memories and wonderful moments. Despite this, I am happy to return to my study in Paris. Living and composing in a city which constantly remains strange to me is the key to an existence which allows me to detach myself from the reality and get into the abstract language of music."[50]

Saariaho also thinks of herself as an introvert who does not seek publicity. "I don't get any satisfaction out of the attention I receive as a composer; however, publicity is a part of this job."[51] In her country of origin she is a well-known public figure who cannot move about without receiving attention. In her opinion, she is "too recognized in Finland. When I say this to colleagues in America, they think it's fantastic that there is a country where composers can be esteemed public persons. In a way it is fantastic, it's true, but that doesn't suit my personality at all."[52]

Over the years, Saariaho has established a supportive group of friends and musicians. She regards working with musicians as the greatest gift of her profession. Karttunen and Hoitenga continue to be her closest collaborators and together with Finnish-born artist Raija Malka, she has created music and art exhibitions, for which she has composed "the musical air for the visitor of the exhibition to breathe."[53] Her long-lasting collaboration with a fellow student from the Sibelius Academy, the composer and conductor Esa-Pekka Salonen, has also been influential. He has premiered many of her orchestral works and conducted performances of her operas. Saariaho praises him for being particularly sensitive to the sound quality, an important aspect of her music. He also inspired her to begin composing for orchestra. "When I began to be interested in computers, I took a break from the instrumental world. Thanks to the orchestral concerts conducted by Salonen, which made a deep impression on me, I began to actively reconsider the possibilities offered by the traditional orchestra."[54]

Interesting comparisons can be drawn between Saariaho's career and music and those of Magnus Lindberg (b. 1958), another internationally known Finnish composer of the Ears Open! generation who continued from the Sibelius Academy to Darmstadt and IRCAM and who has lived in Paris for extended periods of time. Concerts including the works of both Lindberg and Saariaho are always very interesting because their works complement one another; Saariaho's breathing and transparent music is utterly unlike Lindberg's powerful and packed texture. Both of them display highly developed craftsmanship, musical depth, and sense of form.

A close working relationship is born out of mutual understanding, respect, and inspiration. Several musicians have become keen on Saariaho's music and have interpreted it in what she considers to be an interesting and intensive way. This has been the basis for the continuous fruitful collaboration Saariaho has maintained with them. When Saariaho heard the American soprano, Dawn Upshaw (b. 1960), in Olivier Messiaen's opera *Saint-François d'Assise* (St. Francis of Assisi), she wanted to compose for her voice; a couple of her important vocal works, *Château de l'âme* (1995) and *Lonh* (1996), were composed for and dedicated to Upshaw. Upshaw also performed one of the three roles in the first stagings of Saariaho's first opera, *L' amour de loin* (2000). She experiences Saariaho's vocal music as "living in a sound and harmony"[55] more than as particular melodic lines being important in themselves. This suits her well because she is more drawn to the harmonies and to the colors than to the horizontal development. She respects the inventiveness of Saariaho's music, which she senses as taking her "to some new place." Upshaw's bright, beautiful voice and her readiness to explore new sound characters are ideally suited to Saariaho's vocal music.

In the early 1990s, Saariaho began entertaining the thought of writing an opera. She wanted to explore the grand themes, love and death, which "we cannot really approach through reason but that I feel can be approached through music."[56] Gerard Mortier, the director of Salzburg Music Festival, proposed the opera commission to Saariaho after the successful Salzburg Festival premier of *Château de l'âme* in 1996. He introduced Saariaho to Amin Maalouf (b. 1949), a French-Lebanese author with whom Saariaho developed a fruitful working relationship. Both equally fed each other ideas to achieve their shared common goals. "The collaboration with Amin Maalouf has been so easy; we have an intuitive connection, I don't need to say much and he understands what I mean."[57] One of the leading American directors, Peter Sellars (b. 1957), entered the team while Maalouf was working on the libretto. Sellars, a professor at UCLA, is known for his modern stagings of classical operas and plays. His stagings often approach the art as a bridge between humans and the divine, forming a medium for addressing moral and social issues.

When reflecting upon Saariaho's career, writing an opera seems to be a natural continuation of her earlier work. However, Saariaho had been uncertain whether her musical language was dramatic enough for the opera stage until she saw Sellars's productions of Mozart's *Don Giovanni* and Messiaen's *Saint-François d'Assise* at the Salzburg Music Festival in 1998. She understood that opera today in fact can be something very different from the conventional opera, and she finally came to believe her music, too, could work on the opera stage.[58] She also saw what the dimensions of good staging could add to the music; Sellars's staging respected the music, showing how much more there was to the score than just the sound. Saariaho found a soul mate in Sellars, for whom meaningful art touches the transcendent. In his opinion, opera can provide glimpses of spiritual activity inside the simplest moments.[59]

The premier of *L'amour de loin* at the Salzburg Music Festival in 2000 was received enthusiastically. Several descriptions of Saariaho's music and personality were published in the international press. A French journalist, Gilles Macassar, compared Saariaho with Clémence, one of the three characters in the opera, by quoting text by Amin Maalouf, "belle sans l'arrogace de la beauté, noble sans l' arrogance de la noblesse" (beautiful without the arrogance of beauty, noble without the arrogance of the noblesse).[60] Salzburg was followed by successful performances of *L'amour de loin* at the Théâtre du Châtelet in Paris and the Santa Fe Opera Festival in New Mexico. These performances marked Saariaho's final breakthrough and her arrival at the forefront of contemporary composers.

An essential factor in the developing career of a contemporary composer is his or her publishing house and agent. Chester Music, which functions in several countries, including the United States, provides Saariaho's scores and handles the business side of broadcasting, publishing, and performing rights for her works. An important aspect of this work is editing Saariaho's works in preparation for publication, which she does in collaboration with an assistant provided by her publisher. The branch of Chester Music in France is responsible for organizing public relations around Saariaho's music and overseeing new commissions and performances in France. The range of responsibilities is extensive and, to do it successfully, the agents need to have a good network and knowledge of people working with contemporary music. In 2001, at the time of the French premier of *L'amour de loin,* Saariaho was, to the representative of Chester Music in France, a celebrity in Finland, "adored" in Belgium, and well known in France and in other French- as well as German-speaking parts of Europe.[61] By now, Saariaho's music has been performed in the centers of contemporary music both in Europe and in the United States. Her music is published by either Chester Music or Edition Wilhelm Hansen and several record companies, including ONDINE, Sony, EMI, and Petals, have released her music on CDs (see Selected Listening).

At the beginning of the new millennium, Saariaho was decorated with several prizes, the Nordic Music Prize (for *Lonh*) and the Académie Charles Cros, Grand Prix Multimédia (for the CD-ROM *Prisma,* which presents information about Saariaho's career and music) in 2000; the following year, Saariaho received the Christoph und Stephan Kaske—Stiftung prize in Germany and the Rolf Schock Prize in Sweden.

Saariaho's works were also performed by major orchestras. For instance, during the 2002–3 season, among others, the Boston Symphony, Chicago Symphony, Orchestre de Paris, BBC Symphony, and NDR Symphony orchestras performed her works. In 2003, Saariaho was honored by the foremost North American recognition given to a contemporary composer: the Grawemeyer Award (worth two hundred thousand dollars, given by a jury consisting of musical experts and representatives of concert audience) for *L'amour de loin.* Back in Finland, Saariaho was granted an honorary doctorate from Turku University and Helsinki University, in 2003. The keen international interest followed by *L'amour de loin* made Saariaho feel as if though she was "in Disneyland."

When Saariaho was still writing *L' amour de loin,* she thought this would be her only opera, but the collaboration within the team Maalouf-Sellars-Saariaho was so special that when she received a proposition for a new opera commission from Gerard Mortier, the newly elected director of the French National Opera, Opéra Bastille, she could not refuse the temptation to take the challenge. The intensive cooperation between the librettist and the composer, as well as the long rehearsal period including several people who have different approaches to music, provided a welcome change from writing concert music. Saariaho and Maalouf enjoyed the fruits of their previous collaboration. This second collaborative project progressed fluidly and the opera was finished in three years. Thereafter, Sellars—to whom *Adriana Mater* is dedicated—took on the planning and staging of the opera. Saariaho regards the good collaboration as a necessary requisite for opera work. "Perhaps some other composers wrote only one opera because they did not find good collaborators."[62]

Adriana Mater was premiered at Opera Bastille in Paris, in March 2006; its American premier was in August 2008. It describes the scars caused by war and violence in individual lives. It seems that, over the years, Saariaho has become more concerned with current affairs. The collaboration between Maalouf, Sellars, and Saariaho continued with Saariaho's oratorio *La passion de Simone*. The commission was made jointly by the Vienna Festival, Barbican Center in London, Lincoln Center in New York, and the Los Angeles Philharmonic Orchestra by an invitation made by Peter Sellars, who was planning a festival of contemporary art to celebrate the Mozart 250th anniversary in Vienna in 2006. The subject of the oratorio, Simone Weil (1909–43), was a Jewish philosopher born in France, who lived during the Nazi period; she wrote about the divine dimensions of life and worked for the oppressed. By the end of 2007, *La passion de Simone* had been performed also in London, Helsinki, and Stockholm with a planned U.S. premiere in Los Angeles in October 2008.

It would be a mistake to regard the increased social consciousness of Saariaho's work as being solely a result of Maalouf's and Sellars's influence. Such a simple evaluation would overlook the continuous presence of these concerns in her mind, although her expression of these thoughts was minimal in her earlier works. When writing music for *Adriana Mater* she found her own ways of addressing the problems of violence and war in today's world without compromising her art. Saariaho is also deeply concerned about today's musical world, in which the financial benefits are often at odds with artistic goals: "I think these issues cannot be kept out of music. Even in the musical world, I see how the world is becoming increasingly extreme. Musicians and artists receive less, but more is expected from them. The musical mega spectacles have nothing to do with the art. I experience a serious imbalance in these systems."[63]

Saariaho also has a clear vision of the role of contemporary art music in today's world; for her, it is music that includes delicate and spiritual dimensions: "The art music of our time is not elite music but an alternative movement. In a similar way as the biological farming aims at quality without poisons [artificial fertilizers], the task of today's artist is to nurture with spiritually rich art. To provide new spiritual dimensions. To express with greater richness, which does not always mean more complexity but with greater delicacy."[64]

Today, Saariaho is contacted for several commissions a week; she selects those that best suit her current ideas. She also carefully selects the invitations she accepts and the journeys she makes because they take time and energy away from composing and her family. She no longer needs to explore the possibilities of electronic sound because she can easily define the sounds she wishes to produce. Her home studio is well equipped to prepare all electronic parts. Her most important collaborator on the computational and electronic side of her compositions continues to be her husband, but she also relies on the resources of IRCAM for professional help in developing the necessary software and for other practical support.

Thus, the new millennium has seen major developments in Saariaho's career as her music has been brought to new performance stages, resulting in increased international fame and her growing concern about worldly affairs. However, Saariaho does not regard *Adriana Mater* as a political opera or *La passion de Simone* as an oratorio standing with a political message, because she thinks that "political messages are always very articulated and clear and I think a world of art should always allow many interpretations—that is its richness."[65] Despite her own success, she is worried about the future status of contemporary music; in her experience, the position of art music has changed: "If we speak about the circles and instances I move in, in which my music is performed, I would say that it is scattered and really small. If we have to continue to live within the conditions imposed by the market economy I fear that this music which I represent will vanish."[66]

2 Developments

SAARIAHO'S MUSICAL CAREER and musical production can be divided into seven key phases, the first of which covers the period when she was studying at the Sibelius Academy. During this period she was both learning about and looking for composition techniques that would suit her musical ideas. She initially composed vocal works, exploring vocally produced sound qualities, but she soon began to experiment with the electronic means that were available at that time in Northern Europe. Already in the early 1980s, Saariaho electronically processed the sound of acoustic instruments in the concert setting. This early interest in combining electronics with live performance has remained one of the focuses of her attention and one that has developed in tandem with the means of sound processing. The second phase covers her first years abroad. This was an important time during which she sought to define herself as a composer and to find the basic ingredients of her idiomatic musical expression.

The third period could be called the sound laboratory. During this time, Saariaho worked extensively with computers, analyzing different kinds of sounds and becoming familiar with the possibilities computers offered to her compositions. Her emphasis was more on intellectual studies and computerized music than on composing instrumental or vocal music. A characteristic feature of the works from this composition period is a form built up without a regular pulse, which slowly transforms sound surfaces, usually on many levels of the musical texture.

By 1986, Saariaho's instrumental writing with all its colors and notational methods had matured. The timbre period includes an intensive phase of composing, during which Saariaho examined the interconnections between sound color, harmony, and musical forms. This timbre period produced a variety of important works for different kinds of ensembles and electronics, a radiophonic tape work, as well as several other important smaller works for both solo instruments and vocalists. In 1988, Saariaho worked in San Diego, where she concentrated on writing her major first work for symphony orchestra, *Du cristal.* This work shows the culmination of her ideas about timbre, written into orchestral texture.

The timbre period was followed by a transitional period during which Saariaho distanced herself from writing musical transitions. During this stage, she sought musical means to create more dramatic events and abrupt shifts in linear progression. This transitional period in her composing also includes her only ballet, *Maa.*

The following larger orchestral works were already products of a new composition period, in which works are built on identifiable musical gestures. This period of musical gestures emphasized linear developments; for instance, melody gained new importance, at first in her violin concerto and later in a couple of major vocal works. Even though these works certainly stand on their own, they can also be interpreted as practice pieces leading toward writing on a grander scale, as exercises toward the coming large-scale vocal works, the operas and an oratorio.

Saariaho's final and current stage of writing reveals a mature composer in her prime. This dramatic stage in her career began with the production of her first opera, *L' amour de loin,* which also gave birth to other vocal works. They revealed the dramatic sides of intensive, albeit lyrical writing and, with her second opera, *Adriana Mater,* Saariaho moved toward even more dramatic writing: operatic tragedy. A new feature of her production is the way in which it comments on world affairs. "I have the feeling that today's artist carries within him/herself the tradition of humanism in its broad sense. Together, we should take care of this great possession and find ways of keeping it alive—also after we have gone. This task seems to be so difficult nowadays."[1]

Alongside these large-scale stage compositions, Saariaho has also gone to the other extreme and produced smaller compositions. These smaller works force the listener to concentrate on the tiniest, most fragile miniatures of lingering sounds. It is too early to say whether this foresees a new period.

Saariaho's international reception—the reviews of her works in newspapers and music journals, presentations of her music, published interviews, and scholarly writings about her music—has closely followed the different phases of her musical career: early journalism expressed curiosity about the newcomer until gradually she was presented as a promising young composer and, thereafter, as an established composer. The changes in how she has been received by the media clarify both the conventions of art music reviews and cultural variations in music journalism. Her sex and nationality, the two aspects of Saariaho's background that have continuously played a role in her reception, have been seen differently at various stages of her career. Interestingly, Saariaho's sex has played a much lesser role in her international media publicity than during her early years as a rare woman composer in Finland.

Saariaho's music has been remarkably often described with vocabulary that could be called feminine, particularly in Finland; for instance, Juhani Nuorvala characterized her music as "[a] fragile, brilliant play of color, a sensuality, a dreamlike mysterious atmosphere, the female voice and the flute, visual and poetic associations."[2] Thanks to her international success, which is much admired by a small nation, Saariaho's "wrong" sex for a composer was finally "forgiven" and accepted by the Finnish media. In the review of her composition concert given at the Sibelius Academy, in 1998 the music critic Jukka Isopuro reflected upon Saariaho's past engendered reception in Finland: "Kaija Saariaho has successfully managed the label of 'women's music.' Only a few continue to speculate whether her works sound as if they were made by a woman."[3]

In 1993, Saariaho reflected on the influence of gender on the reception of her works, as well as on her own self-esteem as a composer: "For a long time my music was always described as 'by a woman'; very many colleagues gave me this 'compliment' which is: 'I wouldn't have believed this music was written by a woman.' For a long time I must have believed these things too—can a woman really write music which is as good and as structurally powerful as a man's?"[4]

At the age of forty-eight, Saariaho was asked, again, if being a woman has affected her career and she replied: "In the beginning it was a disadvantage, for sure. I was often not taken seriously at all. But is this because I'm a woman or are all young composers treated like that? Later, I've met many jealous colleagues who think it's a big advantage."[5]

Saariaho's career and reception do not support the assumption that a woman composer would receive more attention than her male counterparts. Nor has Saariaho been particularly active in her attendance of concerts and music festivals that only feature works by women composers; quite the contrary, she fears that they "ghettoize" music made by women. Saariaho regards motherhood as a rewarding part of her life that grounds her thoughts in the surrounding reality. "To write music, concentration is necessary, an interior hearing. To be a woman, to be a mother, one needs to be always available and busy—at the same time, you have your feet on the ground and your head in the sky."[6]

Given the international music markets of today and the fact that Saariaho has lived outside Finland for several decades, her works are surprisingly often received as the works of a Finn, Sibelius's compatriot, who comes from a Northern country of snow and ice. The reviews often reflect a kind of imagined Northernness, constructing stereotypical ideas of Northern character, such as coolness and emotional detachment. The associations evoked by music may also be dominated by Northern landscapes; for instance, a review of *Nymphea* (1987) describes how "the scraping noises of the opening pages call to mind the breaking of huge ice blocks on a northern river; a rising and falling rhythm later evokes the rocking of nocturnal waves; and so forth. There are fierce tremolos, eerie rustlings, high metallic screeches, and enigmatic whispers. All fused into a highly charged and poetic totality."[7]

Whereas Northern images dominate reviews of Saariaho's works outside of Scandinavia, the Finnish and Scandinavian media often finds French influences in her works. "In Finland, everyone says my music has a French flavour; in France, they write that this music comes from the bleak north."[8] The Swedish music critic, Lars Hedblad, connected Saariaho's *Graal théâtre* to France, Stravinsky, and Sibelius: "The second and last chapter of the French-elegant work opens to pure Paganiniada. The high fields and light sonorities may lead the thoughts to Sibelius, the agitative expression to Stravinsky. But the sensibility is Saariaho's, only a few can, like her, develop musical energies that are so sophisticated and subtle."[9]

Musical Phases

Saariaho's first publicly performed work was *Bruden* (Bride; 1977),[10] a song cycle for soprano, two flutes, and two percussionists, based on texts by the Finland-Swedish poet Edith Södergran. Saariaho went on to compose other songs using Finnish, Swedish, and Chinese poems, as well as texts by T. S. Eliot. These early songs already used a variety of instrumental colors to paint the atmosphere. One can detect in them also other features, such as long leaps and airy instrumentation, which were to become trademarks of Saariaho's later vocal compositions. Occasionally, the words and their expanded consonants and vowels were also used as musical means. For instance, *Suomenkielinen sekakuorokappale* (Work in Finnish for Mixed Choir; 1989) is humorously built on exaggerated phonetic variations that are typical of the Finnish language The text of the work consists of Finnish names in an alphabetical order.

Laconisme de l'aile (Reticence of the Wing; 1982) for solo flute and optional electronics already presents a highly developed musical expression. The work can also be understood as a development of the musical ideas Saariaho presented in her earlier works, such as . . . *sah den Vögeln* (. . . Saw the Bird; 1981). Saariaho regards *Laconisme de l'aile* as the first work written in, as she calls it, her "own musical language": she had found a satisfying balance between "the means and the content of expression." The flutist whispers a verse of a poem about birds by Saint-John Perse while playing the flute. Although other composers had included spoken words in the works for flute, Saariaho was the first to demand the flutist to recite words while playing.

During her early years in Paris, Saariaho continued to employ the same electronic tools she had used in Helsinki for adding new sounds to instrumental and orchestral music. She also began to develop her harmonic thinking on the basis of computerized sound analysis, and to use the results of these analyses as building blocks for creating harmony and form, devising transitions between the bright sounds and noise. Computers aided her to generate musical material and to create interpolations.[11] Her first composition for tape alone, *Vers le blanc* (Toward White; 1982), used the sound synthesis program Chant developed at IRCAM. The work consists of a smooth transition over fifteen minutes from one three-tone chord to another chord, "sung" by digitally calculated human-like voices while it glides away from the well-tempered chromatic scale. The work evidences Saariaho's fascination with sound when slowed down to its extremes. In *Vers le blanc*, she aimed at creating "music without bodies," voices singing without breathing, which was possible with a computer.

Another work of that period, *Jardin secret I* (Secret Garden I; 1985), is dominated by a slowly moving sound field, the central parameter of which, again, is sound color. In *Jardin secret I*, Saariaho used interpolations to produce musical transitions. Gradual transitions are also the core of *Verblendungen* (Dazzlings; 1983), which consists of tape and orchestral parts evolving in opposite directions along the same trajectory from rough sounds/noise to bright translucent sounds. The work starts in a drowning of the pure sounds of the orchestra with noise from a tape. Over the course of the work, they change places and, at the end of the work, the orchestra sounds like the tape and the tape produces the orchestral-like texture. When preparing early sketches for *Verblendungen*, Saariaho read a book *Die Blendung* (1935) by Elias Canetti, which describes dazzling as a physical and psychological phenomenon. Canetti examines how people can be dazzled by an abstract notion that renders them incapable of perceiving other things. This became the core metaphor for Saariaho's composition. Her first visualization of the overall form of the work was a brush stroke on paper, which evolves from climax to gradually vanishing lines (Graph 1). Saariaho used this form to contest the traditional ideal in which the work develops toward the climax. A CD-recording of the work was reviewed by Mike Silverton: "*Verblendungen* opens with bang, and so did my ears. The composer's command is simply stunning. She's equally and abundantly at ease within both electronic and acoustic spheres. The woman's music makes sparks fly. Moreover, her electronic-acoustic manipulations differ so from work to work that they amount in sum to a tour-de-force. The music speaks harmonically complex, albeit wonderfully accessible syntax—an intricately crafted contemporaneity suffused with grace."[12]

In *Verblendungen*, Saariaho combined for the first time music on tape with live musicians. She produced the raw sound materials for the electronic part from two violin sounds in the GRM studio of Radio France. Later, she compiled the

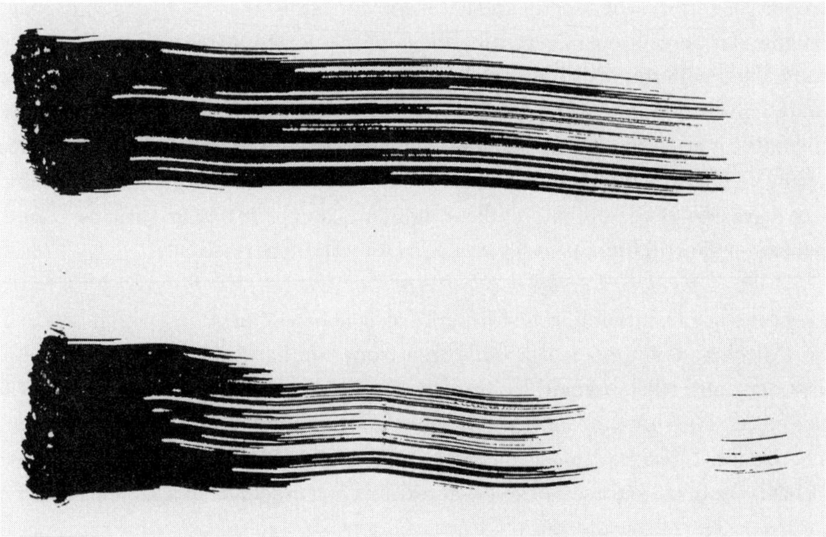

Graph 1: The first visualization, a brush stroke, of the overall form of Verblendungen. *By permission of Kaija Saariaho.*

tape part in the studios of the Finnish Broadcasting Corporation with the help of sound technician Juhani Liimatainen, with whom she continued to collaborate for many years. When working on the tape, Saariaho was already composing the orchestral part of the work. According to Liimatainen, already in the early 1980s, Saariaho treated electronics as simply one of a range of instruments to actualize her musical ideas, employing only carefully selected aspects.[13] In *Verblendungen*, Saariaho also tested her interest in combining electronics—in those days this meant using a magnetic tape—with live music, which she also continued in *Jardin secret II* (1984–86) for cembalo and tape.

By 1986, Saariaho felt that she had found her means of composing and developed her own type of instrumental writing with all its colors and notation. After having worked in studios for a long time, her interests returned to living musicians and their interpretation of music. For *Lichtbogen* (Arches of Light; 1985–86) for nine musicians and live electronics, she analyzed instrumental sounds in order to generate harmonic material and applied, again, computer calculations to create instrumental interpolations. *Lichtbogen* was inspired by the northern lights that Saariaho saw in Lapland in 1984; "Those who have experienced them know the feeling of eternity when seeing the lights moving across the arc of sky gently challenging our perceptions. Everything happens in a perfect silence, which demands to be filled with sounds, colors, and movements."[14] The flute plays the main role on the musical dramaturgy. Due to the amplification, the audience can also hear the flutist whispering phonetic material coming from the French translation of a poem by Henry Vaughan (1622–95), *The World:* "I saw eternity the other night, like a great ring of pure and endless light, all calm as it was bright, and round beneath it time in hours, days, years, driven by the spheres."

Like *Vers le blanc*, *Lichtbogen* consists of intensive but slow progressions of vast musical clusters, building transformational, synchronic passages, which proceed between bright sounds and noise, often from familiar sounds to unidentified, abstract ones; harmony and rhythm are also harnessed to create the timbre of the piece. The slow transitions of transforming sounds are, however, no longer as central as in *Vers le blanc* or in *Verblendungen;* each transformation is different. What is common to these works is that textures rich in sound color are the primary means in the construction of the form of the work.

It is tempting to hear *Lichtbogen* as an auditory form of arches of lights, but this was not the composer's intention. Instead, she was inspired by Vassily Kandinsky's ideas about the power invested in oppositions. She applied his ideas to textures, sonority, orchestration, and the choice of register; the transitions take place between oppositions, for instance, between layers of pure sounds and noise.

In *Lichtbogen*, Saariaho deployed a harmonizer (thickening the texture by transposing pitches with a quartertone up and down). She also amplified selected strings in order to foreground them over the orchestra; thus, amplification becomes a part of the orchestration.

Lichtbogen was greatly praised by the international press, for instance, by Alan Rich from the *Los Angeles Herald Examiner*, in 1989. "The sounds are dazzling. Yes, there do at times seem to be streamers shooting across empty spaces. By her own admission, Saariaho likes to work with noise and at loud volume levels. By 'noise', she means the kind of distorted, otherworldly sounds that come out of the collision of live performance and electronics. Her kind of noise, however, is very sophisticated stuff, because of her brilliant sense, first of all, of timing. Over all, '*Licthbogen*' forms a shapely arch in which strange and marvelous events seem to occupy exactly the right amount of time. I find her music strong and beautifully fashioned, not merely the work of a talented woman composer, but of a talented composer who happens to be a woman."[15] *Lichtbogen* became a classic that is still played today.

Gradual transformations of sound surfaces on several levels of the composition that evolve without a regular pulse were also typical features of the following works of this intensive period: *Io* (1985–87), *Nymphea* (1987), and *Stilleben* (1987–88). The musical expression is nevertheless different; these new works include many dramatic changes. Within a couple of years, Saariaho had moved forward from the static evolving nuances of *Vers le blanc.*

When composing *Nymphea* (Waterlily; 1987) for string quartet, Saariaho used interpolation as her model for instrumental writing. She continued developing musical processes with the help of computers as she did when composing *Lichtbogen*. *Nymphea*'s harmonic structures are also based on the rich spectra of recorded cello sounds analyzed with the computer. Saariaho explored new bowing techniques for the cello and for the strings in general, and Karttunen experimented with some of her ideas about cello sounds to see whether they could be realized in practice. During a performance, amplification as well as such processing programs as harmonizer and reverberation (reflected and echoed sounds) are used. Again, amplification foregrounds very soft sounds that normally remain inaudible.

The work contrasts "limpid, delicate textures with violent, shattering masses of sound."[16] The musical motifs presented gradually converge, only to reoccur in a changed form; the musical texture goes through several rhythmic and melodic transformations. Meetings of different kinds of oppositions play a central role: bright sounds and broken sounds, beautiful pure sounds and noise, and acoustic and electronic sounds. Like *Vers le blanc* and *Lichtbogen*, *Nymphea* also ends with a fading sound as if it would never end: the sounds merely peter out beyond the reach of the listener's ear.

Nymphea is also an illuminating example how Saariaho's sonic ideas regarding deformed, broken cello sounds and sound processing can expand the sounding scale of the conventional string quartet, without completely moving from the tradition. It balances on the fine line between convention and tradition: each instrument in the ensemble plays an individual role as it would in a traditional string quartet, and one can also recognize the typical sonic quality of the string quartet. However, each instrument's scale of sounds is expanded by new playing techniques and live electronics. Varieties of traditional way of playing, such as rapid tremolos, are harnessed into the service of a type of musical progression that builds on delicate sound colors.

The combination of rich sound colors played by traditional and expanded playing techniques with added electronics, producing well-structured and beautifully sounding music, has surprised critics, like Gavin Thomas and Anthony Bye from *The Musical Times:* "The effect of listening through a microscope, of eavesdropping on an inner—and normally hidden—world of sound, one which seems as inevitable as it is original. The application of electronics to extended instrumental techniques may suggest the worst excesses of contemporary music, but what is most striking about this music is its sheer sonic beauty."[17] They regarded *Nymphea* as "Saariaho's virtual reinvention of the string quartet" and "the veils of electronically manipulated sound mixed with hushed, almost inaudible spoken text" of the haunting work as "simply unforgettable."[18] Although *Nymphea* was denigrated by a couple of critics for lacking perceptible structures, there were also those who recognized the multiple operative structures at play in the work. After *Nymphea*, Saariaho wrote her first solo work for cello, *Petals* (1988), "a petal of the waterlily," which is a musical examination of one aspect of *Nymphea* as a kind of afterthought.

In the late 1980s, Saariaho composed a radiophonic tape work, *Stilleben* (1987–88), a piece that is meant to be listened to on the radio. Although radio broadcasting sets certain restrictions on the intensity of events, the work allowed Saariaho to draw on both her vast studio and composition experiences. *Stilleben* is a thematic collage of instrumental and vocal sound sequences as well as concrete, everyday sounds; it also includes spoken and whispered texts in three different languages: Finnish, German, and French. The harmonic material for *Stilleben* grew out of *Lichtbogen*. *Stilleben* includes many sound transformations, for instance, the sound of the metro is transformed into a typewriter. The concrete sounds are often processed by different kinds of electronic filters. And, like in many other radiophonic works, the placing and moving of sounds in the space, stereo, is central; here Saariaho regarded the stereo movement as a musical parameter, not as an effect.

The central theme of *Stilleben* is traveling; it is an expression of the multi-layered process of being within a moment. The composer's sentence, "still life and a moving landscape through the window," guides the listener through this auditory journey. The inspiring first idea was "opening" everything that happens within one blink of an eye.[19] The thoughts in the traveler's mind, the things he sees (the window and aspects of the passing landscape) and hears (fragments of discussions, announcements, and the sounds of the train), intermingle to create a single experience. For musicologist Anne Sivuoja-Gunaratnam, *Stilleben* is a maximal expansion of the idea of transition: the theme of traveling is a transition, non-arrival, and non-fulfillment. The communication between the two persons featured in the work also remains in a transitional state; they never meet.[20] For Saariaho, *Stilleben* is also about longing: "Since my childhood I have been fascinated with, as well as anxious about, the fact that one does not learn to know during one's life time the universe within oneself, not to mention other people, not even one's own children. In Kafka's famous letters to Milena he wrote 'written kisses never come through because the ghosts drink them on the way.' This idea of impossibility to communicate from distance proved fruitful as it allowed me to use rich sound material, sounds of typewriters, telexing machines, trains, and airplanes as well as the languages of my life."[21]

At the end of 1989, Saariaho wished to continue developing the ideas of transformation with new tools: she brought her sonic and formal ideas to the symphony orchestra. When she was writing *Du cristal* (From Crystal; 1989) for orchestra, she even felt the powerful, physical presence of the musicians. At the time, she was expecting her first child and she became aware of having two hearts beating inside her body, at first one of them beating much faster than the other. Over the course of time, the heartbeat of the unborn child grows and slows down until the two hearts have almost the same beat. In *Du cristal,* the fast heartbeats became the ticking pulse played by a triangle, accompanied by a much slower, low pulse played by timpani or bass drum. Toward the end of the composition, the fast pulse becomes slower and eventually finds the same rhythm with the low pulse.

Du cristal was also inspired by the waves of the Pacific Ocean, which Saariaho watched and listened to, counting the varying pulses of the waves, while composing this piece during her stay in San Diego. The music critic, Edward Seckerson, associated the work with the sea and, unlike so many other reviewers he heard nothing "Finnish" in it—whatever kind of "Finland" there was in his mind: "Oceanic is the only word for *Du cristal.* Chiming bells glint from a panoramic wash of sound; piccolos intensify the play of light; deep resurgent groundwells are at once unfathomable. Physically, spiritually, we are light years away from Kaija Saariaho's native Finland."[22]

Contrary to what the title of the work, "from crystal," suggests, Saariaho was not thinking of describing crystal, not even as a metaphor for reflections of life. Instead, she focused on the form, aiming at "discovering the most perfect, most symmetrical ways of organizing musical materials."[23] The orchestral voices, including expanded and unconventional bowing techniques, create extremely integrated and vast living masses of sound. The conductor Esa-Pekka Salonen, to whom the work is dedicated and whose orchestra, Los Angeles Symphony Orchestra premiered *Du cristal*, regards it as a kind of "link from the impressionists to Sibelius. It is a colorist piece, but it's not really neo-anything."[24]

Berlioz, one of the first composers who occasionally built the musical progression on sound color, came in the mind of music critic Barry Millington when he was listening to *Du cristal:* "Berlioz was, in his time, lampooned for the immense forces he unleashed, and for the unprecedented sounds he drew from them. Yet even he might have been stunned into silence by the sight of Saariaho's score for *Du cristal*, with its countless staves packed tight with notation. This is both distinctive and a distinguished score, and provided one is not frustrated by the inability to hear the detail, say, the solo violin near the beginning or even the trumpet later on. It makes for compelling listening."[25]

Du cristal is the highlight of Saariaho's timbre period, which explored sound color as the form-giving parameter in musical transformations and the close relationship between sound color and harmony. In the *Du cristal* and its sister work, . . . *à la Fumée* (. . . to the Smoke; 1989–90), the main emphasis is still on large sound textures: sound masses alternate with glimmering, almost transparent texture. The melody remains marginal and the rhythmic motifs are servants to sound color. In both of these works, Saariaho's sonoric writing for the orchestra is especially captivating because of her way of creating contrapuntal continuums with colors. Interestingly, the instrumental writing in these works includes same kind of ideas regarding sound colors that Saariaho previously realized electronically; she wrote for the orchestra "as if it were a huge synthethizer."[26] The prolonging harmonics—which can also be found in her other orchestral texts—is reminiscent of the spectral composers. To a conventional listener, who anticipates harmonic progression but is not accustomed to paying attention to the sonorically eventful music with constant variations of sound color, the prolonged harmonics of spectral music are a challenge. The structural ideas may remain unnoticed if the attention is focused on harmonic development, as observed by Greg Hettmansberger in *The Daily News:* "[I]t is difficult to discern much difference in approach insofar as 'Cristal' is concerned with a brilliant, fixed substance and 'Fumée' purports to express the elusiveness of smoke. The new work certainly is full of color—frequently clangorous, roaring colors, liberally spiced with a multitude of percussion—but in the course of 20 minutes does little to establish tension and resolution."[27] To perceive tensions and resolutions created by sound color one has to listen differently, with new ears.

When compared to Saariaho's earlier production, *Du cristal* demonstrates a new approach to musical material; melodic fragments gain new emphasis. The names of the sister works, *Du cristal* and . . . *à la Fumée*, "from crystal to smoke,"[28] refers to transformation. Although these works are born from the same musical material, they are distinctly different: *Du cristal* forms large arches of tension and release, whereas . . . *à la Fumée* for alto flute, cello, live electronics, and orchestra includes drastic cuts and abrupt bursts of different instrumental sections. . . . *à la Fumée* includes enchanting interplays between the flute and the cello, both of which employ expanded playing techniques that are further underscored with electronics. Selected soft sounds of the cello and the flute, as well as the whispers of the flutist, are amplified to be in the forefront of the orchestral texture. Saariaho forced herself to compose this kind of more active music after her earlier works with slowly moving textures. Therefore . . . *à la Fumée* marks an important landmark into a new composition period.

Again, a music critic—Andrew Ford from *The Australian Financial Review*—could not resist taking support from national imagery and comparing Saariaho with Sibelius, although he admits that it is misleading to explain her music only in terms of her nationality: "At the beginning of . . . *à la Fumée* you might be forgiven for imagining wintry light shining through a forest of birch trees heavy with snow, particularly if you know the composer's nationality. It doesn't take much imagination to hear this music in the context of glacial landscapes that are Sibelius' Fourth Symphony, *Night Ride with Sunrise*, *Tapiola* and *Scene with Cranes*."[29]

Perhaps surprisingly, Saariaho has written only one ballet so far; the ballet *Maa* (Earth; 1991) was Saariaho's first staged work. Its structure is built on the number seven; it consists of seven parts, each of which is divided into seven sections of different durations and organized in seven different ways. This is not unusual: the structure of almost every work by Saariaho is based on a numeric system; she uses numeric means to outline the proportional durations of different parts of the composition, deciding how much time and musical material they need. She may also decide to build a composition on certain chosen numbers just because the number is beautiful, like number seven, which "divides interestingly unevenly into three and four." The number of instruments used in *Maa* is also seven: violin, viola, cello, flute, harp, harpsichord, and percussion. The seven parts have distinct characters. *Maa* begins with the sounds of (Saariaho's own) active footsteps in differently echoing spaces and surfaces—such as on sand, in the snow, or on wet or frozen grounds—accompanied by a soundscape consisting of concrete sounds. The footsteps create a rhythmic ostinato for the rhythmic material of the whole work. *Maa* also includes other recognizable sounds, such as the sounds of trains, cars, birds, bells, and the sea, which are "tamed" into musical time. Whispers are placed in the forefront of the sounding space to add to the special atmosphere. At the end of the first part, "Journey," a virtual soundscape replaces the concrete sounds; the music, which is freed from the footsteps, evolves into abstract musical structures. The second part, "Gates," is for three instruments combined with live electronics; cembalo, whispers, the bright sounds of the flute, and reverberated cello sounds intermingle within an airy texture. The third part, " . . . de la Terre," written for violin and electronics, is the source of the musical material for the whole work. The violin solo creates musical gestures that reoccur in varied forms. *Maa* combines acoustic instruments and live electronics in various ways; it was also the first work in which Saariaho used a special infinite reverberation that reacts to the loudness of instruments.

In . . . *à la Fumée*, and also in parts of *Maa*, Saariaho tested extreme tempos, unpredictable orchestrations, and progressions set against linear events. These ideas of this transitional period were further developed in the first works of the period of musical gestures. *Amers* and *Solar* (both from 1993) witness a new element in Saariaho's music: distinctive musical gestures that maintain their identity even though they are articulated differently on each occasion. These musical gestures function as orientation markers for the listener, supporting the coherence of the work. Furthermore, the works also have a basic chord to which tensions are released as to the tonic in the tonal system and which is strengthened with a certain kind of playing style. These aspects witness a greater concern for forms based on themes and motifs, even though the harmonic progression in Saariaho's works is never based on tonal thinking: the harmonic structures for these works are found in the same modified spectralist way as earlier, by making computer analyses of interesting sounds and then intuitively creating the harmonic material.

Amers (Seamarks; 1993) for cello, ensemble, and electronics was, again, a success that received only praising reviews. Stephen Pettitt described it as "impressive, tough music," where "[t]here was a vastness and a mystery about it, connecting it to Sibelius, however different the language. The work's inner motion derived largely from sounds enveloping and overlapping each other. [L]istening to the work as a study in colour was probably the best approach at first meeting, yet one was conscious of the sense of organism behind it. Each instrumental element—soloist, small ensemble and computer-generated sounds—constantly tugged at the others, pulling them from their intended path."[30]

Amers was inspired by a poem by Saint-John Perse (1887–1975). The name of the work refers to the navigational markers on the shore used to guide sailors. *Amers* is more lyrical than its predecessors, and it includes more melodic fragments—possibly due to the role of the cello as "the navigator on the sea." The work includes two parts, the first of which presents the musical material in a rigid form, whereas the second plays more freely with this material. The basic chord for *Amers* was created from the same cello trill that ends *Du cristal* and begins *. . . à la Fumée*. Intuitively constructed chords from the analyzed microtonal overtone structure of this trill provide the harmonic structure for this new work. The basic chord for the work functions as a kind of returning tonic chord in the musical progression: it begins both the whole work and the part in which electronics join in. In the electronic part of *Amers*, Saariaho used tuned resonating filters; the harmonic structure of a sound can be modified to correspond with the characteristic harmonies of the whole work. Thus, the work is based on structures and proportions that originate in its musical material. *Amers* is a fascinating combination of concentrated and focused music with unexpected rhythmic and sonic variations. According to the music critic Andrew Clements, from *The Financial Times*, "*Amers* could be admired for the fastidious selection of its material, the delicately graded and controlled textures, the unexpected harmonic shifts and rhythmic collisions."[31]

According to the musicologist Ivanka Stoianova, *Amers* relates to the instrumental concerto tradition. However, as a work without separate movements, it can also be comprehended as a kind of symphonic poem of our time. Stoianova observes how *Amers* combines multiple playing techniques of the cello as well as both instrumental and electronic parts: "By joined manipulation of the exploration of timbre, linear writing, homophony and polyphony, Saariaho creates a complex structure based on fusion and unity, and creates a bridge between timbre and harmony, and between instruments and electronics."[32]

Later works of the 1990s, such as the violin concerto *Graal théâtre* (1994) written for Gidon Kremer, further demonstrated Saariaho's discovery of a new way of writing in which linear elements and recognizable gestures play leading roles in the musical progression. *Graal théâtre* was inspired by a play by Jacques Roubauld about the knights of the round table.[33] Although the legend is old, the text is written in contemporary French and in the author's personal style, which encouraged Saariaho to adjust the tradition of violin concerto to suit her own style. The concerto form allowed musical explorations on a new, theatrical field; it provided Saariaho with an opportunity to work on the relationship between melodic line, harmony, and orchestration, as well as on the interplay of the violin and orchestra. She maintained the fragility of the violin sound, untouched by electronic expansions. The dramaturgy of the work builds on battles between extreme contrasts, not only on the level of its two parts, *Delicato* and *Impetuoso*, but within them. One of the numerous contrasts is between "floating" events and directional melodies.

New Stages

By the mid-1990s, the human voice came to assume greater significance for Saariaho, who wanted to investigate more thoroughly the emotions that only vocal music can evoke. Already at the beginning of the decade she had began to develop the melodic aspect of her music while retaining rich timbral variations as a central element. This desire produced *Château de l'âme* (The Castle of the Soul; 1995) for soprano, eight female voices, and orchestra, as well as *Lonh* (Afar; 1996).[34] While preparing for the opera, Saariaho wanted to experiment with the idea of a vocal line against an electronic background: the result was *Lonh*, in which the soprano sings to an electronic background, consisting of elements recorded on a hard disk and sounds processed in real time. *Château de l'âme*, which has no electronic part, was an experiment that demonstrated how her multiply expressive vocal text fits into orchestral texture. In an opera, the music is forced by the time of staged drama and the orchestration has to allow the sung words to be comprehensible. *Château de l'âme* was her first vocal work with an orchestra. Traces of its, as well as *Lonh*'s, vocal idiom can be heard in the first opera.

Saariaho's idea for *Château de l'âme* was to explore different dimensions of love. The work can also be interpreted as an exploration of womanhood, woman's earthiness and spirituality, as well as her relations to her lover and to her child. The complete text moves from unrequited love to a celebration of motherhood, to a mother's spells and prayers for the protection of her child. The music consists of a wide-spinning, elegant soprano part in a kind of polyphonic dialogue with the whispering and spelling female voices as well as of the exquisite colors produced by the orchestra. It supports the text with gentle tones and with darker colors in steady pulses reminiscent of heartbeats. *Château de l'âme* is first and foremost a vocal work: the female voices dominate at the expense of orchestral complexity.

It is an incantation of inner womanly thoughts and feelings that awaken mystical dimensions of womanhood.

Château de l'âme lasts only twenty-three minutes yet consists of five songs, the relative lengths of which Saariaho indicated in her composition sketches as 4–5–3–2–6, in respective order (Graph 2). The first three songs are based on ancient Indian Vedic texts. The text of the first and third parts, *La liane* (The Liana), describes a romance: "As the liana holds the tree wrapped in itself, so embrace me: be my lover and do not tear yourself from me!" The first part, a prologue, is characterized by upward leaps and downward scales sung by the soloist and echoed by the female voices. The second part, *à la Terre* (To the Earth), has a stable and loving atmosphere. Saariaho made a text collage on the basis of Vedic texts that describe the earthiness of motherhood, the bountiful Mother Earth: "Breasts of gold, the vast earth, brown, red or black, your body, the earth is a mother" (Graph 3). Upward instrumental scales mark the beginning of new verses for the strongly vibrating soprano line, reflected by shimmering instrumental colors and female voices. The third song, a variation of the first Veda, grows into a stormy cry. The last two parts are based on Egyptian magic spells. The fourth song, *Pour repousser l' esprit* (To Deflect the Spirit), is an intensive mantra for the protection of the child;

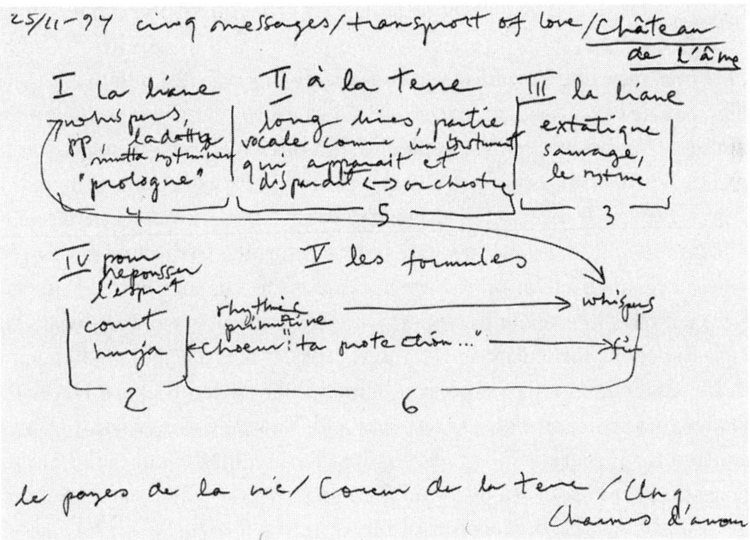

Graph 2. Sketches of the relational proportions (4–5–3–2–6) and overall contents of the different parts of Château de l'âme *in French, in English, and partly in Finnish. Part I is described as "charged but rhythmic"* (ladattu mutta rytminen); *Part IV, as "wild"* (hurja).

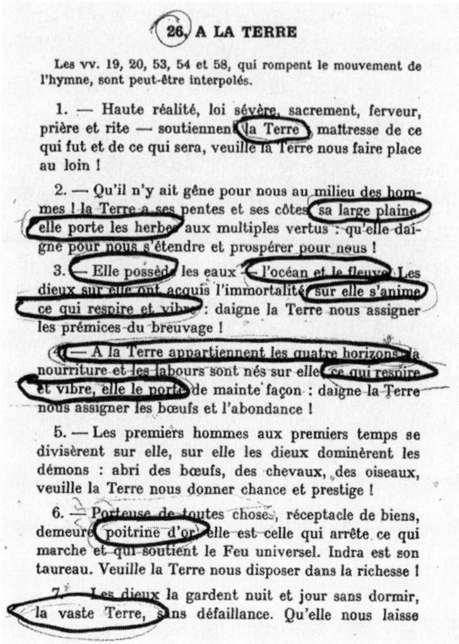

26. A LA TERRE

Les vv. 19, 20, 53, 54 et 58, qui rompent le mouvement de l'hymne, sont peut-être interpolés.

1. — Haute réalité, loi sévère, sacrement, ferveur, prière et rite — soutiennent la Terre, maîtresse de ce qui fut et de ce qui sera, veuille la Terre nous faire place au loin !

2. — Qu'il n'y ait gêne pour nous au milieu des hommes ! la Terre a ses pentes et ses côtes, sa large plaine, elle porte les herbes aux multiples vertus : qu'elle daigne pour nous s'étendre et prospérer pour nous !

3. — Elle possède les eaux — l'océan et le fleuve. Les dieux sur elle ont acquis l'immortalité, sur elle s'anime ce qui respire et vibre : daigne la Terre nous assigner les prémices du breuvage !

4. — A la Terre appartiennent les quatre horizons, la nourriture et les labours sont nés sur elle, ce qui respire et vibre, elle le porte de mainte façon : daigne la Terre nous assigner les bœufs et l'abondance !

5. — Les premiers hommes aux premiers temps se divisèrent sur elle, sur elle les dieux dominèrent les démons : abri des bœufs, des chevaux, des oiseaux, veuille la Terre nous donner chance et prestige !

6. — Porteuse de toutes choses, réceptacle de biens, demeure, poitrine d'or, elle est celle qui arrête ce qui marche et qui soutient le Feu universel. Indra est son taureau. Veuille la Terre nous disposer dans la richesse !

7. — Les dieux la gardent nuit et jour sans dormir, la vaste Terre, sans défaillance. Qu'elle nous laisse

Graph 3. The words and meanings chosen by Saariaho from Hymnes et prières du Veda *(Atharda Veda 6.8). By permission of Kaija Saariaho.*

it is strongly accentuated by the veiling female choir. It ends in orchestral *tutti:* "Are you here to take the child from me? I will not allow you to take her!" The final song, *Les formules* (The Formulae), praises the divinity of the child in a lingering way. The female choir plays an active role. The beautiful lines of the soprano end in glissandos: "Your hips are the coupled vases from which Nile springs, your toes are reptiles. There is no part of you lacking divinity." The work ends with gradually vanishing whispers. It forms a full circle: it develops from the quiet contemplation of the beginning into a passionate state before returning to distant stillness.

The successful premier of *Château de l'âme* at the Salzburg Festival paved the way for Saariaho's first opera to be performed on the same stage five years later, although the openly articulated womanliness of *Château de l'âme* challenged the critics. Its "erotic imagery to express religious feelings" led Richard Dryer from *The Boston Globe* to recall *Song of Solomon* and New Age dimensions, although he admitted that "there is far more texture, density, intelligence, and emotion in this music than in some of its popular counterparts."[35] Christopher Schluren, who reviewed *Château de l'âme* for a Finnish music journal *Rondo*, managed to hear in it Sibelius, French mentality, and Finnish mystical forests; he regarded it as a step toward Sibelianian direction. "The French brightness and lightness combines with the deep forests of Tapiola. The composer finds her 'dream paths' in between these contradictory worlds."[36] Allan Kozinn from *The New York Times* asserted that "[l]ike many of Ms. Saariaho's works, *Château de l'âme* is driven by both an alluring chromaticism and an idiosyncratic lyrical style. Her writing for the solo voice is often understated, particularly because its unpredictable angularity. But just when the soprano line seems likely to fade into the orchestral fabric, Ms. Saariaho invariably gives it a twist that magnifies its intensity."[37]

When looking for a theme for her opera, Saariaho came across a book about medieval legends, *La fleur inverse* by Jacques Roubaud.[38] It included a brief biography of a medieval troubadour, Jaufré Rudel. Saariaho researched Rudel's historical background using materials from the Parisian Bibliothèque Nationale, where she found Rudel's *vida,* his story, written in the fourteenth century, a hundred years after he died. The old, fragile pages of the centuries old *vida,* which includes a fragmental notation of Rudel's song, made a strong impression on her. The theme, love from afar, and one text of Rudel's songs written in a pre-French Occitanian dialect became the main elements of *Lonh* and later also of the opera *L' amour de loin.*

The lyrical *Lonh* consists of a vocal part sung by a soprano into an electronic soundspace, which represents the imagined acoustic surrounding the poem. In the performance situation, the audience sees only the singer on the stage while the three-dimensional electronic soundscape envelops the listener in a virtual garden that accompanies and reacts to the lyrical soprano solo. The vocal line is the core of the work. By the end of the 1990s, Saariaho no longer regarded musical space as an active supporting parameter in musical texture. She had learned that listeners tend to perceive spatiality of music holistically and that the composer cannot control the spatiality of different kinds of concert rooms.

The electronic sound material of *Lonh* provides both an enlargement of the singing voice and an accompaniment to it. It consists of recorded singing, speech, and whispers in Occitanian, French, and English; the sounds of bells, gong, and other synthetic percussion instruments; as well as the sounds of the sea, wind, rain, and bird song. Many of the sounds are sampled and filtered. Saariaho set these sounds into the space with the help of the spatialization program developed at IRCAM; the soprano sings into the resulting soundscape that surrounds the audience. The soprano soloist starts the nine electronic soundscape sequences with a pedal. Her voice is also a subject of live electronics: it is amplified and combined with different kinds of echoes in differently resonating spaces created with the spatialization program.

Lonh is a work in nine parts, each of which has a distinct character. The work is structured on the nine verses of the *vida;* each new section of the work starts with a new verse. The way Saariaho reworked the original text of the *vida* illuminates her ways of treating texts, although she naturally does not have only one clearly definable way of using literary texts. Instead, she searches for individual solutions for each work. Texts that raise her interest are transformed into musical elements; "when I read a poem, I have great difficulties in distancing myself analytically from it. Poetry suggests a similar kind of mystery as music."[39] The language of the text—its rhythms, intonations, pauses, and accents—influences the music; each language produces a different kind of music. This fact, familiar to every composer, may well be stressed in music dominated by sonority; Saariaho carefully utilizes the sonority of words, vowels, and consonants as musical elements of her works.

Saariaho often revises the original texts to suit her musical purposes. In *Lonh*, like in *Château de l'âme*, she used only fragmentary parts of the text although the theme of the poem—the longings of a young maiden on a spring day—influenced the composition. Everything she wished to say with the composition is in the first verse of the poem: "When the days are long in May, the sweet song of the birds from afar seem lovely to me. And when I have left there, I remember a distant love. I walk bent and bowed with desire, so much so that neither the song nor hawthorn flower pleases me more than the icy winter."[40] It was the only complete verse of the original text left in the work. Since the complete poem was too long and had too many words to be fitted into the music, Saariaho selected words and phrases to create meaningful collages. In the composition process, she simultaneously worked with the text and with other material, by fitting the text into the musical ideas and vice versa, by feeding the music with ideas gleaned from the text. The poem also influenced the structure of the composition, which has as many parts as the poem.

In one of her composition sketches, Saariaho described the vocal part as "the soprano like a bird, returning motifs"; the arcs of the vocal line imitate the routes of the flying birds. The few harmonic parts in the electronic background are based on analyses of recorded vocal sounds. The medieval modality provides a fragrance to the harmonic whole; the minor third of the original medieval song appears in *Lonh* as well as in the opera, *L'amour de loin*. Even though the vocal melody has some harmonic meeting points with the electronic background, it remains clearly separate because it is based on a mode rather than on harmonic thinking.

The music critic John Story found in *Lonh* the same feeling as in the heavily ornamented troubadour song, which "tells of a profound sadness recalled at a distance." However, in *Lonh*, the song is created in a different, original manner: "The diatonic vocal line sounds medieval in the context of the glittering mobile of electronic sounds that surround the voice, but, in fact, it uses all the vocal colors available to the 20th century diva from speech to full-throated operatic singing." He regards "Kaija Saariaho [as] one of the most interesting composers currently active. Whatever formal device she uses to actually compose her music, the sensation of listening to it is a kind of free association in which each sound unit leads to the next by a process that can only be described as instinctual."[41]

Oltra mar (Across the Sea; 1998–99), seven preludes for the new millennium for orchestra and mixed choir, also provided material for the first opera. Even though the choir participates in each part, it sings with words only in alternating parts. The texts—titled Love, Death, and Time—are, in the same order, an Arabic poem written by Abou Said, a death song by an African ethnic group, and a section from a novel by Amin Maalouf, the librettist of *L'amour de loin;* "they all speak in their own way about the sky and the planets, as well as human feelings and ideas."[42] As its magnificent themes suggest, the work has a mysterious, greater-than-life atmosphere. It is dominated by the orchestra's large sound masses but the listener's attention is also drawn toward the sound colors, created by both instrumentation and powerfully expressive male and female voices. *Oltra mar* is reminiscent of the gradually transforming sound masses Saariaho created in the 1980s, but it includes new elements, such as musical gestures and new kinds of variations in sound color and vocal texture. Saariaho used ideas developed for *Oltra mar* in the fourth act of the first opera, which describes a voyage across the sea.

The beginning of the new millennium witnessed a significant turning point in Saariaho's career. The first opera *L'amour de loin* (Love from Afar; 2000) began a new, dramatic period in her production and her career entered a new stage. *L'amour de loin*, which is a musical presentation of the emotional process of a distant longing and love growing into mature love, was premiered at the Salzburg Music Festival in August 2000. The world premiere was greeted enthusiastically by almost every critic. David Murray from *The Financial Times* wrote that "*L'amour de loin* is a strange idyll in suspended time: not, certainly, a repertoire piece, but a rare and rather magical experience."[43] Wolfgang Sandner from *Frankfurter Allgemeine Zeitung* regarded it as "ein bemerkenwertes Operndeput,"[44] a significant opera premiere, although he wished that the opera had ended when the male character Jaufré dies, without following the spiritual development of its heroine. The length of the opera, two hours without a break, led H. D. Pribil from *Wiener Zeitung* to wonder whether the opera had been even more powerful if it would have been shorter, although he also praised Saariaho's music, which "impresses through its bright, shimmering, waving, vibrating sound colors, which is reminiscent of both French impressionism as well as Messiaen. The live electronics was also used—but all the time in a sparing way which never brought technique in the forefront."[45] According to Shirley Fleming from *Musicalamerica.com*, "[t]he orchestra, with electronic elements blended so subtly within its texture that one is hardly aware of them, has great luminosity and at times—particularly during instrumental interludes—can be massively rugged, with its solidity punctured by bright pinpricks of piccolo or oboe."[46] A music critic from *The New York Times*, Anthony Tommassini, praised the opera as "a haunting and resonant work—Mr. Maalouf's words invite music, and Ms. Saariaho has provided a lushly beautiful score, structured in five continuous acts lasting two hours. Best known for her explorations of sound, Ms. Saariaho continues in that vein here with music that combines vivid orchestration, the subtle use of electronic instruments and imaginative, sometimes unearthly writing for chorus, which sings from the side of the stage. The vocal writing is by turns elegiac and conversational."[47]

At the end of 2000, Tommassini named *L'amour de loin* the best new opera of the year,[48] and Humphrey Burton from *BBC Music Magazine* was of the same opinion. Burton praised especially the two last acts, which "inspire in Saariaho a sustained vein of agonised lyricism that I found intensely moving. I wasn't alone; there were standing ovations at every performance. Not since Madam Butterfly has there been such a touching depiction of a woman's ecstasy and grief."[49]

The widely praised premiere of *L'amour de loin* increased Saariaho's international stature in Europe. Music journalist Hilary Finch from *The Times* described the scene in the United Kingdom in late October 2001: "everywhere you turn, Saariaho seems to be in earshot. A new disk of three key works, *Château de l'âme*, *Amers* and *Graal théâtre* has recently been released on Sony; tonight her electro-acoustic *Solar* radiates from Birmingham; and in November Saariaho features as a major composer in the Huddersfield Contemporary Music Festival and as composer-in-focus at the London Philharmonic."[50]

Within five years, *L' amour de loin* had been performed in numerous different arenas: in the following year at the Châtelet Théatre in Paris and in the Opera House of Bern; a year after at Santa Fe Opera Festival in New Mexico; in 2003, it was performed also as a new stage version in Darmstadt, Germany, and as a concert version over the years in Amsterdam, Brussels, London, Lebanon, Strasbourg, Berlin, and Paris; and again it was performed on the opera stage in Helsinki, Finland, in 2004 and 2006.

Robert Spano, who conducted the American premier of the opera in Santa Fe, described its sound world as "inviting and sensual. The sort of restated medieval music that runs throughout the opera [links] to chant, to certain medieval practices. It's an entirely new sound world. This world is so elegant and pristine and at the same time, so expressive and rich."[51] The reviews after the American premier in 2002 had no reservations. Shirley Fleming from *Musicalamerica.com* encapsulated several essential dimensions of the opera—sound colors, consonant harmonic language, spiritual atmosphere, and medieval flavors—with a few sentences: "Ms. Saariaho fleshes out the simple story with sounds that are typical of her current style: luminous washes of iridescent color, a haunting dreamlike ambience, a focus on timbre and harmony, and a kind of slow-burning spiritual fire. Though the score cannot be called tonal, its harmonic language hits the ear as hypnotically consonant. Ms. Saariaho occasionally evokes an antique flavor with the struck harp arpeggios of troubadour music, rhythms of medieval dance and modal harmonies tailored to each of the three characters."[52]

Cori Ellison stated in *The New York Times* how the "luminously scored" opera "appears well on its way to becoming one of the stand-out music dramas to emerge in recent memory." In her ears, Saariaho's vocal lines "sweep and soar, dip into sadness or rise to anguish and urgency," while the chorus "reproaches, advises, chants, or breathes a single held note." The sound of the orchestra ranges, in her opinion, "from the translucent to the shattering, and never intrudes unduly while the characters are singing."[53] A couple of weeks later, James R. Oestreich from the same newspaper regarded the opera as the main event of the Santa Fe Opera: "The music is a marvellous fabric, full of nervous energy yet glacial in its movement. Planes and points of sustained sound are adorned with lyrical effusions, wisps of melody, flourishes and 'spins,' as Ms. Saariaho calls certain circular figures."[54] And when reviewing the DVD documentation of *L'amour de loin* made at the Finnish National Opera, Alex Ross from *The New Yorker* praised the "magical immediacy" of the opera: "Saariaho's music captures with magical immediacy the drastic emotions that swirl around this romance, which is different from standard operatic melodrama in that the action is largely psychological. Saariaho's stroke of genius is to keep the melodic lines spare and directly admit the orchestral phantasmagoria; Debussy's *Pelleas and Melisande* is her vocal model."[55]

American performances of the *L'amour de loin* brought Saariaho's works to many concert halls in the United States. Within a couple of years, they were performed by major orchestras and performers at different music festivals, such as at the Ravinia Festival in Illinois and at the Tanglewood Festival in Massachusetts, as well as by major symphony orchestras in several cities, including Boston, Cleveland, Los Angeles, New York, Philadelphia, and Washington.

The first work Saariaho completed after *L'amour de loin* was *Sept Papillons* (Seven Butterflies; 2000) for solo cello, commissioned by the Rudolf Steiner Foundation. She composed it during the opera rehearsals in Salzburg. This work of ten minutes includes seven miniatures studying the fragile movements of the butterfly.

The music critic Justin Davidson admired Saariaho's way of treating the cello "like a microphone, rendering the butterfly's wings as a percussive trill, the fingers of the left hand beating loudly on the fingerboard while long, bowed notes sound like tiny contrails blown up large."[56] The soft, sensitive nuances of the cello in *Sept Papillons* are not amplified as they would have been in Saariaho's previous works of ten years earlier, for instance, in . . . *à la Fumée.* Instead of amplifying the soft sounds and foregrounding them in the musical texture, Saariaho challenges the audience to concentrate and to listen more carefully. The sounds "are left into their fragile position—requiring sensitising of hearing" which, for Saariaho, is "a metaphor for one's life line which so easily gets broken."[57] This new way of respecting soft sounds and tiny details and presenting them in purely acoustic form had already begun in *Nocturne* (1994), which was dedicated to the memory of Witold Lutoslawski, and it continued both in the flute concerto *Aile du songe* (2001) and in *Dolce tormento* (2004), a small work for piccolo that is related to *Orion* (2002).

A child of the first opera, *Cinq reflets de L' amour de loin* (Five Reflections on Love from Afar; 2001) for soprano, baritone, and orchestra, exposes the dramatic sides of the lyrical opera. Saariaho also developed musical materials from the opera further in *Quatre instants* (Four Moments; 2002) for soprano and piano, as well as for soprano and orchestra, which she wrote for the Finnish soprano Karita Mattila. Tim Ashley from *The Guardian* described Mattila's powerful interpretation of this erotic piece: "Setting poetry by Amin Maalouf, *Quatre Instants* examines the emotions of an unnamed woman as erotic anticipation gives way first to inexplicable sexual terror, then to an ecstatic depiction of lovemaking. [Mattila's] voluptuous tone darkens into neurosis as the woman rails at her lover's absence. Sexually assailed by him, she repeatedly rasps the phrase 'remorse burns me' in her chest register, punctuating it with shrieks, at once orgasmic and terrified."[58] Pierre Gervasoni from *Le Monde* predicted that *Quatre instants* "will surely become a core work within the repertoire of the 21st century. The music ceases to be subliminal and becomes the transmission of real-life."[59]

On the North-American concert stages, Saariaho's works were often combined with works by other Finnish composers and performed by Finnish musicians. In 2002, Tim Page described how "Washington seemed a sort of 'Little Finland'—at least the Kennedy Center where a disproportionate number of visiting musicians came from that beautiful Nordic country."[60]

During the first years of the new millennium, Saariaho was more productive than ever, producing one major work after another. Within the space of six years, she wrote a flute concerto (2000–2001), her second opera *Adriana Mater*

(2003–5), an oratorio *La Passion de Simone* (2005–6), and a cello concerto (2006), all of which were positively received. While working on the vocal lines of her first opera, Saariaho had noticed that her way of writing for cello and flute had begun to resemble her writing for the voice: a stronger melodic thinking had come to play a more important role also in her instrumental writing. The flute concerto *Aile du songe* (2001) was written for Camilla Hoitenga after *L'amour de loin*. Saariaho wished to return to her favorite instrument. "For me it was important to find a delicate, transparent texture that was sufficiently varied. The concerto, as well as a few other works that followed the opera, move along the boundaries of silence seeking power from the clarity and depth of the idea rather than from physical energy or great sonority."[61] Musically, the concerto builds around the flute solo, which exploits the sounding universe of the flute to the extremes. For John von Rhein from the *Chicago Tribune*, it was the best piece of new music he heard in 2002: "Saariaho has produced a sound world that shimmers with beauty and wonder. The two sections are filled with images of birds in flight—at once living things that mediate between sea and land, and metaphors for the mysteries of life. Rising in intervals suggestive of Asian musical scales, the flute's avian whistles and flutterings draw delicate responses from instruments of the orchestra, primarily exotic percussion."[62]

Orion (2002) is Saariaho's first work for a big orchestra alone after *Du cristal*. With its tree movements—*Memento mori* (Remember, We Must Die), slow and linear *Winter Sky*, and energetic *Hunter*—it may be closest to the symphonic tradition in Saariaho's production so far. The image of the hunter comes from the Greek myth of Orion, in which a mortal hunter is sent as a radiant constellation by Zeus to the sky. The mortal and heavenly dimensions of the Orion myth are painted with richly colored musical textures, which employ the instrumental palette of a symphony orchestra enriched with the organ and the piano, to the fullest. The musical texture is rhythmically extremely rich and in the third part even playful. Like many works by Saariaho, *Orion* also ends with sounds gradually vanishing in the air; although the tempo increases, the volume and the number of the instruments decrease toward the end.

For Saariaho's continuation as an opera composer, the inspiring teamwork of *L' amour de loin* was crucial. To date, the Saariaho-Maalouf-Sellars team has completed three major productions taking her work onto new stages: the second opera *Adriana Mater* was premiered in Opera Bastille in Paris in March 2006, and the oratorio *La Passion de Simone* in Vienna in November 2006. These pieces introduce an element of social concern within Saariaho's production: *Adriana*

 Mater is about individual tragedies, motherhood, and violence during war, and *La Passion de Simone* is based on the life story of the French activist, author, and philosopher Simone Weil, who sacrificed herself because of her strong social consciousness. The work was premiered in Vienna during Mozart Festwochen as part of the program of the New Crown Hope Festival designed by Peter Sellars.

Only a few contemporary operas have been staged in major opera houses and, before Saariaho's *L' amour de loin* none of them has been composed by a woman. The success it gained raised high expectations: the premier of *Adriana Mater* was attended by music critics and opera directors of the major opera cities around the world. *Adriana Mater*, with its highly dramatic, even brutal theme, received contradictory reviews. Some reviews praised it as a powerful drama that addresses current issues in a timeless and humane manner, whereas others criticized its lack of the essential elements of the theatrical art. Alan Riding from *The New York Times* noted how "[a] story of such intensity demands music of equal power and to judge by the enthusiastic response of the Opéra Bastille's packed house at Monday's world premier, Saariaho succeeded in forging a work on an emotional scale rarely heard in contemporary opera. The opera's changing moods are defined by richly varied orchestration, explosive and reflective, as well as by the urgent parlando and lyrical arias of the vocal parts."[63] In contrast, Francis Carlin from *The Financial Times* regarded the libretto as "banal" and thought that the listener should be "a fervent supporter" of the Saariaho style to overlook the flaws of the opera: "Adriana tries to tackle a more physical world and fails. Saariaho cannot juggle with theatrical pace and timing."[64] And again, Olivier Olgan from *La Tribune* praised *Adriana Mater* as a startling symphonic poem full of delicate sounds and harsh harmonies, which sinks the listener into "an endless melodic stream."[65] A German critic, Jörg von Ülhermann from *Die Welt*, recalled the virtuosity of the orchestration in *L'amour de loin;* in his opinion, the richness of orchestration, which only a few other contemporary composers are equal to create, was the winning card of the new opera as well. "[Saariaho] sets in the ear in a pleasant way—also when she tests the boarders of tonality. What is missing is the rhythmic many-sidedness."[66]

After the premiere of *Adriana Mater*, Alex Ross from *The New Yorker* summarized his experiences of Saariaho's large-scale works in the most illuminating and poetic way: "[They] begin with a great, heaving expanse of intermingled timbres, like a landscape turned molten, or an ocean boiling. Instruments cry out at high or low extremes; pitches are bent or broken apart; violins are bowed with such intensity that they groan; flutes are blown until they emit an asthmatic rasp. It's the kind of sound that boxes the ears and maxes out the brain; information pours in on all frequencies."[67] He stresses, however, that Saariaho is not a sonic terrorist, who aims at shocking the audience. Instead, "[s]he makes her eruptions of noise seem like natural phenomena, the aftermath of some seismic break. Shapes emerge from the chaos, and the shapes begin to sing. The latter sections of her pieces often being apparitions of rare, pure beauty—plain intervals that sound like harmony reborn, liminal melodies that disappear the moment they are heard."[68]

3 Work

IN SAARIAHO'S EXPERIENCE, a composer does not choose her musical style, but the style comes to her. She speaks about having a "musical language" and for her each of her works is a world of its own. In her opinion, being honest with oneself is the only way to create an individual musical expression. When her personal musical idiom dictates the paths she takes, her musical explorations cumulate in unique and consistent ways. She has consistently remained within her own musical vocabulary, although she continuously searches for new musical expressions. Her music naturally relates to the musical and technological developments of her era, but her applications are original. She composes music within the Western art music tradition using traditional instruments and applying resources created by the latest technology. At the same time, she questions and expands musical conventions.

Saariaho's process of composing, as well as her musical production, reflect her personal way of perceiving the world. Different senses intermingle; she senses visual, tactile, and even bodily sensations musically with sounds. Music may also give rise to visual and bodily experiences. She regards this as one of her fundamental ways of imagining music. "I cannot separate these things [musical and visual dimensions] from each other and, in my opinion, one should not even attempt to do so. This differentiation is based on the traditional view, but I am quite convinced that, in addition to the eye and the ear, there are close relationships between the other senses. The senses must not be firmly delineated. Although music is what interests me most and my ways of expression are musical, I do not think of these things as separate categories."[1]

Her composition work often departs and develops from multisensory sensations. The art theorists and artists whose ideas and works have inspired Saariaho, and to whom she feels close, usually have similar kinds of a multi-artistic view of art.

Saariaho has been called a visual composer because many of her works evolve from a visual idea, drafted by herself, from nature, a painting, or a film. Colors, both visual as well as sounding colors, are vital to her experiences and so timbre is a central parameter within Saariaho's musical production; "emphasizing the world of sound colors is a part of my personality."[2] Similarly, many of her works have a literary sister, be it a poem or a piece of prose. These literary and visual sources may be reflected in the title of the work, even though the work never attempts to literally re-create its antecedent. Although the relationship between the title and the music tends to be more metaphorical than denotative, the title and other inspirational sources connected with the work unavoidably affect the listening experience. For Saariaho's composition work, the title functions as a focal point that provides both the context and the direction for the musical material in the composition.

Saariaho regards the work of a composer as a kind of craftsmanship because it involves skills that can only be learned through practice. However, it also includes another part that is inseparable from the craftsmanship: "the whole internal world with its visions. [The composition work] is extremely concrete and disciplined although the result is abstract."[3] Saariaho's career as a composer as well as her everyday working habits bear witness to her persistent hard work, which includes in-depth studies of sound, composition techniques, instrumental and vocal techniques, computer programs and programming, as well as electronic sound synthesizing and processing tools. This diligence results in a constantly developing output.

"When one writes music for instruments, one is giving advice to the musicians [about] what, exactly, they have to do at each moment. In order to be able to do this one [the composer] has first to know the instruments, not to mention the notational traditions, the history and most of all, the composition techniques. Composing is about organising sound and endless decision-making. One has to find and develop methods to limit and mould [musical] materials and methods which produce the kind of music one wishes to create. Composition includes enormous amounts of thinking work and yet, the most important elements develop beyond the realm of conscious thought."[4]

Since music is an art that proceeds in time, time is one of the central components in composition. The composer not only places the sounds into the continuum of time, she or he also consciously creates the impression of time passing in the listener's perception. The impression of musical time usually differs from the real time, which has passed. Saariaho notes how "[m]usic is purely an art of time, and the musician—with or without a composer—builds and regulates the experience of the speed of time passing. Time becomes matter in music; therefore, composing is exploring time as matter in all its forms: regular, irregular. Composing is capturing time and giving it a form."[5]

Unlike many other composers who emphasize the abstract autonomy of musical works, Saariaho does not try to avoid drawing connections. In the program notes, she often describes the literary or visual impulse that led her to compose the work and may have provided both the title and the focal point for the composition. She also sees the connections between her own life and her works: "everything I experience and live, I absorb into myself and there my musical thoughts also originate."[6] Many of her works are biographical: for instance, in an early work, *Preludi—Tunnustus—Postludi* (Prelude—Confession—Postlude; 1980), she chose texts describing love as a battle, in which the one who loves less is the stronger one. Another example is the radiophonic work *Stilleben* (1987–88), which is about traveling and longing, familiar elements in Saariaho's life during those years. Her later works also contain such elements: *Du cristal* (1989–90) relates to the birth of her son. *Château de l'âme* (1995) is partly about her feelings of maternal love after her daughter's birth, and one of the themes of the second opera, *Adriana Mater* (2006), is a mother's concerns about her growing son.

Skillful musicians greatly inspire Saariaho, and so she has written several works for specific musicians. These include *Graal théâtre* for Gidon Kremer; *Château de l'âme* and *Lonh* for the voice of Dawn Upshaw; *NoaNoa* and *Aile du songe* for the flutist Camilla Hoitenga; and several cello compositions, *Petals, Spins and spells, Près, Sept papillons,* and *Notes on Light,* for Anssi Karttunen. Recently, Saariaho has worked ever more intensively in collaboration with musicians and other artists.

Saariaho's musical production reflects the development of musical technology, particularly electronic music. The technology involved in electronic music involves a large—and ever more developing—world of its own. In order to be able to utilize the electronic means available, the composer has to acquire and maintain an impressive working knowledge of how the technology functions and a detailed understanding of the sounding alternatives they can achieve. Early in her career, Saariaho composed tape music, as well as combined tape parts with acoustic ensembles or works for solo instruments. In addition to instrumental and vocal sounds, her works include concrete and processed recorded sounds, synthesized sounds, as well as instrumental and vocal sounds that are electronically processed during the performance. The latter, also known as live electronics, has been a common feature of Saariaho's works since the mid-1980s, when it became technically easier to electronically manipulate music produced by musicians in real time during performance.

Composition Process

During the working process, rational work, such as sound analyses conducted with computer programs, alternate with intuitive decision-making. As a composition student, Saariaho used to analyze the works of other composers in order to learn composition techniques and to find inspiration for her own work. Today, she seeks out solutions from within herself. For Saariaho, the greatest pleasure in the composition process arises from the feeling of being inside the process and from the certainty of taking, undisturbed, her own route to achieve a musical creation. Anssi Karttunen, who has followed the work of his friend for several decades, believes that "ultimately, there is such a sense of inevitability in Kaija's music that while she naturally controls the material, the material by its elastic nature controls the music. Kaija's music is such a perfect mirror of her personality that you cannot tell where one ends and the other begins."[7]

When considering Saariaho's persona as the primary inspiration for her music, there seem to be two aspects—her Finnish background and her multisensory sensations—which cast light on her musical world; "the most important thing in my perception is that the visual and the musical world are one to me."[8] Saariaho perceives the world and makes associations—also musical thoughts—through several senses that blend together in the experience. "Different senses, shades of colour, or textures and tones of light, even fragrances and sounds, of course, blend in my mind. They form a complete world in itself, which calls me to enter into it, and where I can then focus on some details. They are the source from which I draw."[9] Sounds and different sonorities relate to smells, colors, and textures. This kind of multisensory perception, known as synesthesia, has been discussed in relation to the composition work of György Ligeti (1923–2006), Messiaen, and Sibelius, as well as artists, for instance, Wassily Kandinsky (1866–1944). Synesthesia means that information perceived by one sense is involuntarily joined with a perception by another sense. In addition to being involuntary, this additional perception is regarded by the synesthete as real rather than imagined.[10] Saariaho has also explained how "[s]ounds, events, scents, colours and dreams twist into each other—my world has been like this as long as I can remember."[11]

The multisensory perception sometimes also draws on physical experiences. *Verblendungen* (Dazzlings; 1982–84), for instance, has its roots in Saariaho's childhood experience of feeling the warmth of sunlight on her skin; "When I listen to music and when I imagine my music, there are also coloristic aspects [involved]—I am not looking for these relationships between images and sounds but they exist in me."[12] When asked to verbalize the ideas she has expressed through her music, she says that "they are powerful blends of certain atmospheres, connected to nuances of colour, sometimes clear instrumental combinations, or some kind of flickering between two musical emotional states."[13]

Several works have been born from either visual or literary impulses that have triggered Saariaho's musical imagination. For instance, the northern lights provided the impulse for *Lichtbogen* (Arches of Light; 1985–86), and *Nymphea* (Waterlily; 1987) was inspired by different kinds of materials—earth, water, air, and wind—fusing together in the water: the plant's roots in the mud, the stem that brings the leaf to the surface of the water, and the flower that reaches toward the sky.[14] Nature also functions as a source of formal thinking. "I am very interested in the structures found in nature—especially the symmetry of leaves and flowers. I am working on transforming such patterns musically. There are patterns within nature and colors or musical timbres within which these patterns lie."[15] This contact between the physical and the musical has interested several philosophers and composers before Saariaho. For instance, Arnold Schopenhauer discussed how "[m]usic differs from all the other arts by the fact that it is not a copy of the phenomenon, or, more exactly, of the will's adequate objectivity, but is directly a copy of the will itself, and therefore expresses the metaphysical to everything physical in the world, the thing-in-itself to every phenomenon. Accordingly, we could just as well call the world embodied music as embodied will."[16]

The primary impulse for *Près* (1992–94) for cello and electronics came from Paul Gauguin's painting *By the Sea*, which links it, in Saariaho's mind, to the experience of the sea and the waves, their different kinds of rhythms and sounds, on stormy and calm days. In musical terms, these sounds and rhythms refer to different kinds of musical materials and the textures, shapes of musical forms, rhythmic figures, and timbres; these factors are used to charge up the music and to release that charge. In *Amers*[17] (1992), which is the sister work of *Près*, the visual images are, unusually for Saariaho, musically presented. The work was also inspired by pilot markers on the shore guiding the ship, and the ensemble and electronics represent the sea. According to Saariaho, the cello soloist "seeks a passage through the sea of sound like a seaman steering his ship."[18]

The sea is a reoccurring element in many of Saariaho's works. However, she does not aim to directly re-create the sea or its waves through her compositions, nor is she interested in the symbolism of the sea; her interest is in the "interesting noise" and pulse of the waves. Sounds, however, can also be figurative, if they are associated with a natural form or if they are recognized as concrete sounds. In regard to this aspect, the relationship between the abstract and the figurative is what Karttunen finds interesting in Saariaho's music, particularly the moment of transition from the abstract to the figurative. "[While playing] I don't think of real waves, rather about the form of waves. At first the sound of the waves is recognizable, it represents the idea of a wave which gets closer to the real sound and finally you recognize the natural sound. The important moment for me is when the sound changes from abstract to figurative."[19]

Birds and bird song are also recurring elements in Saariaho's compositions. For instance, the visual inspiration behind *Laconisme de l'aile* (1982) for flute and optional electronics is "the lines which flying birds draw in the sky."[20] The bright sounds of bird song are wholly unlike the noise of the sea and the sound of the wind. These kinds of dichotomies of sound are also important in regard to the musical form of Saariaho's works. The sound of the wind is unpredictable; it does not have a pulse like the sea. Saariaho has also used several recorded natural sounds as musical material. The semantic meanings of natural sounds do not interest her; she never attempts to transmit the meanings to music. Sometimes this evokes interesting associations for the listener, who hears the sounds as parts of the work (for instance, footsteps in the ballet *Maa*) simultaneously recalling their meanings (walking up the stairs).

Saariaho perceives sound colors more as qualities of luminosity than as colors as such, although she experiences—conventionally, in her own opinion—the sounds of brass instruments, such as trumpet and trombone, as warm colors and horns as softer, warm red colors; the woodwinds as a section produce colder colors and the sound of the violin is yellow. The color of the instrumental sound depends on many other musical aspects, for instance, texture, orchestration, and register. When composing, Saariaho attempts "to work on the continuity between the experience of the ear and the eye."[21] She is particularly interested in liminal states, when something changes into something else.

Saariaho's own musical thinking and the terminology she has developed for categorizing musical sound colors, such as *rough*, *smooth*, *bright*, and *clear*, refer to non-auditory sensations. She uses these categories when constructing her works, but they also open up a way of listening to her music. Sometimes Saariaho's own bodily sensations serve as the inspiration for a composition. "In some ways I experience the relationship between the body and the mind as the same as the relationship between form and content, as inseparable as the material and the form of a piece of music."[22] She has also used her own recorded voice, whispers, and footsteps as material for her compositions.

The inspiration for a work is often born from a strong momentum given by a natural phenomenon or an artistic work, painting, film, or poem. The basic character, in Saariaho's vocabulary, a *tone* or a *smell* of the work, arises from the first impressions and the thoughts evoked by them. For instance, her experience of examining *Water Lilies*, painted by Claude Monet, was material for *Nymphea* (1987).[23] The starting point of *Nymphea* is a musical exploration of the complex character of a singular natural phenomenon, a water lily. It explores the flower's visual form, colors, and materials and how it can respond to changes in the light. It details its relationship to the elements of earth, water, and air as well as reflects upon the "sensed" essence of the plant itself. In the concert program, Saariaho describes some of the images that evolved in her mind when she was sketching the piece: "the image of the symmetrical structure of a water lily, yielding as it floats on the water, transforming. Different interpretations of the same image in different dimensions; a uni-dimensional surface with its colors, shapes and, on the other hand, different materials that can be sensed, forms, dimensions; a white water lily feeding on the underwater mud."[24] *Nymphea* also provides an excellent piece for illustrating Saariaho's synesthetic musical thinking. Initially the image and sensing of the water lily are transformed into a purely musical expression, but once one has heard the music, the flower takes on new meanings as one becomes aware of its visual, metaphorical, and spiritual essence.

Saariaho has also combined ideas originating in the visual arts with her musical thinking; she thinks of the forms, structures, and characters of musical and visual elements in the same terms. "I would like the visual part to be as composed, as detailed, as the music. In fact my thinking is very visual, my sketches are drawings for a lot of pieces and I always wondered whether they would also work for something visual."[25]

The theories of Johann Wolfgang von Goethe (1749–1832), Wassily Kandinsky, and Paul Klee (1879–1940) were influential for young Saariaho. Goethe's theory of colors, particularly regarding the liminal states of light and shadow, are reflected in Saariaho's interest in slow musical transitions. "I read from Goethe's *The Study of Colors* something about the liminal states between light and shadow.

The thought of slowing down of speech to the extreme, when a vowel changes into a consonant, is similar. The borderline is usually so small that we do not perceive it. There is something significant in it."[26]

Kandinsky was a painter who related visual arts with music; he explored relationships between sound and color and described his paintings as "compositions" and "improvisations." Saariaho especially admired his paintings from the period 1913–17, when he broke away from figurative work to experiment with abstract forms. Kandinsky's thoughts regarding forms built on oppositions between the point and the line have been especially influential on her musical thinking. For Kandinsky, the essence of art is not in external forms but in its internal content; the form is an external manifestation of the internal meaning, which also determines the material. The spirit dictates the material and not vice versa.[27] These ideas can be discovered in Saariaho's way of transforming the impulse-giving momentum to works of music. Her approach to the "living sound" can also be related to Kandinsky's approach to colors as constantly moving phenomena.

Paul Klee's influence may be detected in a number of Saariaho's works where she creates a musical expression of the internal forms of natural phenomena. Klee aimed at explaining the forms of nature, seeking out relationships between the internal state and the external surface. According to him, the harmony between the internal and the external raises the question about the spirituality of the intellectual form.[28] He also explored the regularities of movement in nature, which influenced his understanding of form and space; harmonic, static space provides the point of departure for dynamic development. In his works, the static and dynamic correspond with certain painting techniques. In Saariaho's works, they are elements of musical structure.

Other art forms also inspire Saariaho's musical ideas. For instance, when watching a film, she may discover a solution to a current musical problem.[29] Some films, such as *Stalker*, an impressionist film directed by Andrei Tarkovsky (1932–86), and *Dans la ville blanche* by Alain Tanner (b. 1929) have been particularly influential on her music; for instance, *Stalker* had such a great impact on Saariaho that in 2000, when she had a chance, she wanted to visit the old factory outside of Tallinn, Estonia, where the film had been shot.

Saariaho is an avid reader of literature; she seeks suitable texts for her vocal works. Some texts remain on her desk until she feels that she must compose them. She only composes those texts that move her or reflect her own experiences in some way. The literary sources come from various literary traditions, from medieval scripts, Western novels, and non-Western epics. An even closer connection to visual art can be found in the works she composed for art exhibitions, such as

La Dame à la Licorne (The Lady and the Unicorn; 1993) for the art exhibition of Raija Malka; the ballet *Maa* (1991), which was a co-production with dancer-choreographer Carolyn Carlson; and *From the Grammar of Dreams*, a visualized staged performance.

Saariaho's musical work never aims to simply paint or describe the text, painting, or natural phenomenon that has inspired the work. *Nymphea* does not aim at describing either water lilies in general or Monet's painting by the same name; *Lichtbogen* does not present a musical illumination of the northern lights, nor does *La Dame à la Licorne* musically paint the content of the medieval tapestry with the same name in the Musée national du Moyen Age—Thermes de Cluny in Paris.[30]

Saariaho's works musically grasp the Gestalt, the essence of the primary source. She transforms the same impulse that inspired the painter or author of the original work into music or, in the case of natural phenomenon, she transforms its revelation into a musical form. "Music comes in small bits or large ideas or directly as sounds to the composer's mind. Sometimes I ask myself whether music is brought about by the friction between the musician and the surrounding world, or rather from the energy tapped from nature and other arts? In my specific case, maybe the latter, maybe both. I also feel that smells, light, and colors are a wellspring of musical ideas."[31]

The preliminary impulse, a multisensory experience or an association, often provides the title of the work, stating its main mental character. Further along in the working process, the title functions as a focal point for the composition process. The preliminary impulse of the work also dictates the choice of musical material. Thus titles help Saariaho define the musical material which, according to her, is the most complicated part of composing. For the listener, the title of the work functions as a point of reference for the perception or even as a key to understanding the work. The title may also entice the listener to enjoy the same spiritual essence in the original piece of art, in another art form, or in nature.

For Saariaho, composing is about imagining abstract music and deciphering it into a score. Sensations and images function as ideas for the main characteristics of the work, not as determinants of the musical elements. Karttunen has observed how Saariaho's composing process proceeds: "from the very abstract it transforms into the visual and, finally, to the musical."[32] From the title of the work she moves next to visual sketches of forms from which she gradually works in details by making technical decisions. "Each work consists of sentences that somehow relate to each other and eventually tell a story. This story does not have a concrete meaning, but it is a kind of narrative with its own logic."[33]

The process of composing includes detailed technical work with intuitive openness. Saariaho begins working on the basic idea of the composition by drawing visual sketches of the different aspects and parts of the work. "My sketches for many pieces are drawings. But even if a visual phenomenon strongly inspires me, it gives me musical ideas which are finally abstract."[34] The most illuminative example is the brush stroke she drew when making plans for the formal structure of *Verblendungen* (see Graph 1). It was the last work for which she created the harmonic material before starting to use computer programs for this purpose.

Saariaho's harmonic material is rather limited and, therefore, recognizable. "For me, harmony is like a fragrance—either you have it or you don't have it. If you have your own personal harmony, the listener perceives it at once, and it characterizes the music. If a composer does not have her or his own harmony, it is for me music without an odor."[35] Saariaho has a specific method, which relates to spectralism, to develop harmonic material for a new work. For example, for *Lichtbogen* (1985–86), she analyzed the overtone spectra of selected recorded sounds with a computer program in order to create the harmonic material for the work. The program not only identified all the pitches involved in the sound, it also selected the most important ones for the perception. From this information she then intuitively chose the pitches for the basic chord around which she finally organized the harmony of the work. Unlike spectral composers, Saariaho does not necessarily stay within the physical sound spectra; she may freely add to it by transposing or using permutations. This factor makes her composition technique different from that of spectral composers, who stay within the physical characteristics of the sound.

After Saariaho has chosen the harmonic principles, she draws a kind of harmonic map of the whole work and develops the other musical materials. She makes decisions about the instrumentation and she sketches different kinds of textures, sound colors, and playing techniques, as well as makes plans for the rhythmic characters of different parts and melodic gestures. Saariaho may draw sketches on graph paper in order to map the proportional durations and characteristics of different sections of the work (Graph 4). These visual sketches are not informative for an outsider, but they help Saariaho recall the basic idea and characteristics of the work. The aim of these sketches is to document the holistic impression, a kind of "mental essence" of a section. They consist of visualized musical forms, drawings regarding the density of musical texture, written characterizations of the main aspects of the work, remarks concerning rhythm and tempo, harmonic models, partial notations, as well as notes on instruments and orchestration. The verbal comments also indicate the character of the musical gesture. Making these sketches enables Saariaho to uncover details in the work, which gradually develop

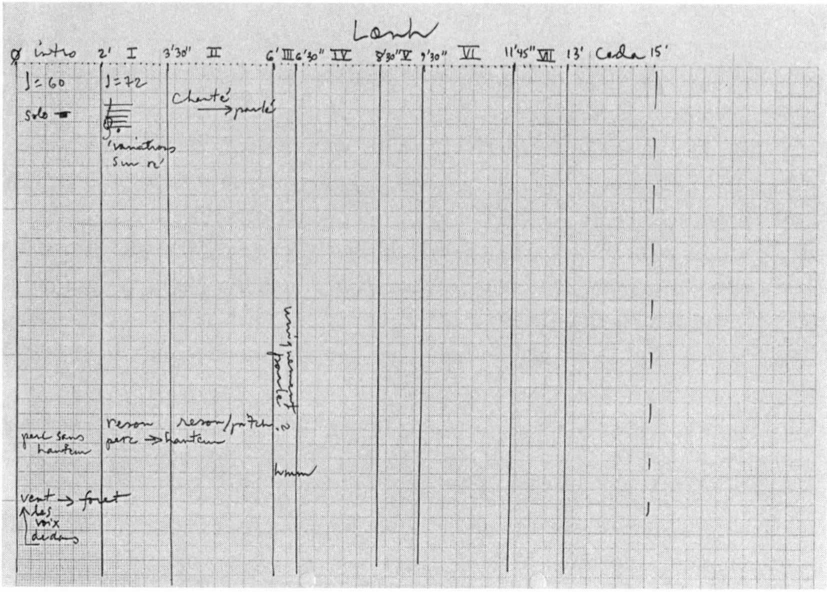

Graph 4. Temporal dimensions of different sections in Lonh *sketched on a graphic paper. By permission of Kaija Saariaho.*

from visually sketched abstract ideas into musical phrases. Over the course of the composition process, these verbally, visually, and only partly musically sketched abstract ideas are worked into musical gestures and details.

After having drawn several primary illustrations of different parts of the work, Saariaho sets them into the complete structure of the work. The formal foundations of a musical work may be based on numerical structures, changes in the dynamics, or characteristics of music; usually it is a combination of several different aspects.

The form of Saariaho's composition is always created together with musical material. She never forces the material into a traditional musical form, but creates the form from the material. "The form is not a cake mold into which you pour your dough but, rather it directly relates to the material."[36] She aims at composing directional musical processes. Each element relates to the others; "the form is born from the character, the form creates the character, the character determines the instrumentation which, in its turn, provides ways of dealing with the form and the material."[37] The work evolves as a network of interrelated dimensions. Thus, no general principle covering all Saariaho's works exists, instead, each of her compositions has its own hierarchy of musical parameters, in which certain chosen aspects dominate others.

For the musical material, Saariaho likes to combine natural, electronic, and instrumental sounds, without placing them into any hierarchical order. It is important to her that the musical material consists of "vividly living sounds" because she finds most stereotypical electronic sounds uninteresting. An instrumental sound is always a living sound, but electronic sounds can become interesting only if they are constantly varied.

If the work includes electronic sounds, it may require collaboration with studio technicians in order to realize Saariaho's ideas. Studio work involves close collaboration between the technical assistant and the composer and so a shared vocabulary for describing the sound world is needed; the terminology used by the composer comes from his or her training, whereas the sound technician commands the technical terminology. In the course of the project, the composer and the technician may develop joint terms for certain sound events.

Saariaho never draws the first note before she has finished sketching the work in its entirety, in regard both to its structure and to its details. She has the need to know the totality of the work before she starts composing it; she writes her compositions using the traditional notational system, primarily because musicians who play her music are used to it. She finds it miraculous that the notational system that has been used for centuries can still convey the latest musical ideas. Since no standard means of notating electronic music has been established to date, composers have to develop their own system that suits their music. However, this must be comprehensible to the musicians. If a work combines some form of electronics with acoustic performances, Saariaho adds indications of essential characteristics, such as changes in the dynamics or harmonic structures of the electronic part, in the musicians' score. The work also includes a technical score for sound technicians. Saariaho's way of notating the electronics is relational, because the sounding result always depends on the concert room.

Saariaho hardly ever plays or listens to the music while composing it because computer programs cannot simulate different kinds of playing techniques, which is such an important aspect of her music. For her, it is more fruitful to imagine the music in her mind. She even imagines the physical movements of the instrumentalists. "When I compose in my studio I imagine the gestures physically, however, without touching the instrument. I wait for the first contact with the musician who finally creates the work."[38]

She defines the preliminary tempo markings when making the first sketches of the work. In the final work, the tempos are often marked in approximations, because she wishes to provide space for the musician's interpretation and for his or her personal tempos. This is particularly important for singers and their personal voice formation. Relative durations and tempos are more important for Saariaho than a controlled, accurate tempo. Characterizations, from *calmo* to *furioso*, are defined in detail in Saariaho's scores; sometimes different instruments have contrasting characterizations.

Saariaho's score may, at first glance, seem to be filled with several different kinds of simultaneous information and difficult details, such as constantly changing tempo markings and scales and additional advice. Saariaho also notates aspects such as changes in timbre and sonority as well as detailed vibratos and other playing techniques. Such scores are demanding for musicians who are unfamiliar with her musical thinking. Once a musician has learned to read the notation as well as the required playing techniques, she or he notices that the notational system is extremely clear and logical and that Saariaho's music consists of climaxes and releases, like any other work of Western art music. Her works are clearly structured and build on directional moves. Even though the score includes a great deal of information, it is only a referential picture of the music that allows much space for interpretation. Saariaho leaves room for the musician to "live and breathe" with the music.

Esa-Pekka Salonen has observed how professional musicians learn to interpret the technical or notational details of Saariaho's music. In his opinion, Saariaho's way of notating her music, including special playing techniques and variations in the sound color, is so self-evident that they can read it without great difficulty. However, her music is unlike anyone else's, and musicians have to become familiar with its special character. Once a group of musicians has performed a piece by Saariaho, they grasp the effectiveness of the broad musical landscapes and the intensity of the living sounds provided by her works.

Up to 1991, Saariaho enjoyed the sound of the scratches of the pencil on paper as she wrote her music by hand. She wrote the works twice, initially creating the primary score, which she revised and transcribed again. Her handwritten works are beautifully grafted. Today, Saariaho still continues to draw sketches by hand before writing music with computer and adding graphic signs indicating timbral variations and playing techniques by hand on the printouts. Saariaho's assistant transfers these markings into computer files.

Saariaho is not a composer who revises her works several times. Once she has written the double lines, her work is usually complete. There have, of course, been some exceptions. For instance, she revised the second part of . . . *a la Fumée* several times before she was satisfied. She also adjusted the soprano part in *L'amour de loin* and revised her violin concerto, *Graal théâtre*. Updating the technological elements of the old works also requires constant revision. This time-consuming task is one of the reasons electronics play a smaller role in her more recent compositions, but the more important reason for using less electronics is that she is ever more concentrated in working together with musicians.

The feedback Saariaho receives from skillful musicians is vital for her. Collaboration with trusted musicians, especially when expanding ways to use traditional orchestral instruments, has often been an important part of the composition process. Both the musicians with whom Saariaho has worked most intensively—Karttunen and Hoitenga—emphasize that when working with them, Saariaho is not seeking out new musical ideas but is trying to find the optimal technical realizations of her existing musical ideas. They do not usually discuss works while Saariaho is composing but only afterward, when the first version is ready.

Electronic Dimensions

As a composer of her era, Saariaho has, throughout her career, utilized electronic sound processing tools and computer programs in her composition work. She employs computers and other electronic tools in the composing process, in her works, and in their performances. She makes microscopic analyses of sounds that interest her in order to find musical, particularly harmonic material for the work; she synthesizes sounds and processes prerecorded concrete and musical sounds; she creates virtual soundscapes and modifies existing sound spaces. Live electronics (processing in real-time sounds produced by musicians during the performance) also play a central part in her production.[39] In Saariaho's music, electronics are never used just as an effect, but as an organic part of the musical language as well as a form-giving element of the compositional structure.

Saariaho has combined electronics with acoustic music since the early stages of her career. For instance, *Verblendungen* consists of simultaneous orchestral and electronic parts, and in *Jardin secret II* the cembalo is accompanied by a tape background. Most of her production, however, adds an enchanting electronic dimension to instrumental or vocal music by complementing or modifying the music of the acoustic performance in real time. Some of her works, such as the orchestral works *Graal théâtre*, *Oltra mar*, and *Orion*, have been purely instrumental, while others, such as *Vers le blanc*, *Jardin secret I*, *Stilleben*, and *La Dame à la Licorne*, are purely electronic works. Electronic means of producing and modifying sound have never been Saariaho's major interest; although she has been involved in inventing new sound technologies, technology has never been a goal in itself.

Saariaho's production reflects the development of music technology over three decades. When she sought for ways to extend the musical expression of traditional orchestral instruments, ensembles, and the human voice, she even developed, in collaboration with others, a few new technical solutions, such as an infinite reverberation and harmonic filters. In this respect, she follows in the footsteps of the futurists of the 1910s, who defined music as the "art of noises" and began to use all possible, particularly technological, means of producing sound. Interestingly, almost every way of using electronics together or without acoustic music that is used today was already discovered during the early years of electronic music. Technological development has simply provided more defined means for creating electronic music.

Synthesizers, invented in the late 1960s; digital sound, the product of the 1980s; and the rapid development of computers have greatly furthered the integration of electronic sound into the Western art music canon.[40] Highly developed means of recording, producing, and modifying sounds provide contemporary composers, such as Saariaho, with unlimited sound resources, from recorded sounds to synthetic sounds, including all their possible combinations and variations. According to the music historian Robert P. Morgan,[41] one of the consequences of this development has been that the border between music and noise no longer exists; noise has become a significant compositional element—as can be heard in Saariaho's music.

Saariaho's multifaceted capacity as a composer is also evident in the electronic parts of her compositions. As a composition student, she was initially interested in timbre and sound synthesis; she learned to analyze sound spectra and found her own way of using selected pitches from the overtone structure when creating the harmonic material of the composition. Saariaho records interesting instrumental, vocal, or concrete sounds and analyzes their overtones with the help of computer programs that can select from the rich database the most important pitches for perception. She may also analyze a transition from one sound to another, for instance, from the pronunciation of a vowel to a consonant, in order to reveal the rich sonorities of the process. From the analyzed material, she chooses suitable pitches for the harmonic material. This allows her to use those microtonal structures and measure-relations that are inspired by the content of the material. It enables her to compose organic musical works, which combine timbre and texture with harmony, color, and pitch.

Saariaho's aesthetics in regard to sound color have been greatly influenced by her investigations of sound. The computerized analysis and modification of sound challenged her to consciously define factors involved in the creation of a new work, factors that had previously been determined intuitively. This did not come naturally to her, but she found it a fruitful task in regard to her compositions, as well as to the conscious and unconscious processes of musical creation. The analyses of sound also taught Saariaho much about the timbral qualities of music. She learned about the harmonic potential of the sound spectra and about musical organization.[42] Saariaho's experience of working with computers and electronic tools has also influenced her writing for the orchestra. According to the music journalist Andrew Clemens, "the shifting layers of some of [Saariaho's] impressive orchestral pieces would have been unthinkable without her knowledge of electronic music, just as the highly detailed scoring would not have been possible without her punctilious analysis on a computer of the harmonic components of instrumental music."[43] Paul Nelson, who has analyzed Saariaho's use of electronics in shaping her composition, has noted that they make the form clear to the ear in the same way as in the more conventional music.[44]

Saariaho has always used both synthesized sounds and processed sounds in her works. Over the years, she has become very selective when choosing from the large range of possibilities that electronics can provide for sound synthesis, which, for her, is just one instrument among others. She has been particularly interested in expanding the sound color as a directional continuum of the sound of acoustic instruments, and as a follow-up to this, she has taken interest in developing musical interpolations (a composition technique that creates either stage by stage or continuous changes from one musical character to another). In 1993, Saariaho stated that these ideas, including sound analysis, were involved in every work in which she had used synthesis.[45]

Sound processing is used to modify the frequencies and temporal dimension of sound and, consequently, the character of the sound. The most typical methods of sound processing for Saariaho are harmonization and reverberation. With the harmonizer, Saariaho may transpose one pitch a quartertone up and another down, which considerably thickens the sounding texture. She particularly uses the harmonizer to create textures of noise. Several of her works include sounds that have been processed with the harmonizer. Reverberation, the adding of reflections of a sound to its original form, was a common element in Saariaho's earlier production, but currently she uses it more sparingly. Reverberation extends the sound both in time and in place; it is used to increase the sound's duration as well as to create virtual spaces and change the impressions of actual spaces. If the sound of a live performance is reverberated, it may also echo in the background while the instrumentalist keeps on playing. In this way, reverberation can even be used to create polyphony. The echo may also be placed in an unending loop, which extends it into a kind of *borduna* sound for the melodic or sonoric progression.

Saariaho initially began to use amplification because she wanted to make the soft sounds and the tiny details of sound processes heard. Amplification echoes, expands, and freezes sounds, thereby changing the impression of space.[46] If a soft sound of a performance is amplified, it may dominate other sounds in an acoustic performance; in this manner, the amplification changes the natural hierarchy of volumes. Saariaho also uses reverberation to alter the natural order. "The more silent the sound is, the longer the echo should be" is her advice, for instance, in regard to the electronic part of *Petals* (1988). Under natural circumstances, the stronger the sound is, the longer the echo should be.

A smaller work, *Près* (1992–94) for cello and electronics, provides a good example of Saariaho's way of using electronics to expand the sounding scale of the cello. It grew out of ideas that became familiar in the cello part of *Amers* (1992). The musical material of these works is the same but used within different kinds of forms and dramatic structures. Only a couple of instrumental passages and electronic elements are the same. In *Amers*, the electronic part functions as a bridge between the cello and other instruments, whereas in *Près* the electronic part is an extension of the cello, in regard to both sound color and musical gestures.

The electronic part of the work[47] expands the cello sound, on the level of both sonority and musical gestures. *Près* includes both synthetic sounds and modified cello sounds on the disk, as well as real-time sound processing made by resonant filters and different kinds of echoes (reverberation) and transpositions. The synthetic sounds are based on recorded cello sounds; Saariaho analyzed their overtone structures, which she then used as the basis for the harmony of the work. The same analyses were also used for the basis of sound synthesis, which became the direct-from-disk material incorporated into the work. The synthetic sounds were realized using resonant filters, which also operate in real time in certain passages of the work. Saariaho aimed at creating a work in which the amplified cello sound, in spite of the many layers of progression, stays in the forefront of the listening experience. The direct-from-disk component provides both a kind of accompaniment and a playing partner rather like in chamber music for the solo cello.

Près has three movements, the first of which, *Misterioso*, presents the musical material, in Karttunen's words, as "a perfect, static world."[48] The cello is played, at times, with overpressure, which transforms the sound into noise. The never-ending echo (reverberation) added by the computer creates the impression of a sound vanishing into the cosmos. Toward the end, more electronic effects are added to the cello sound, including a number of sounds direct from disk. The second part, *Agitato*, introduces new elements for both the electronics and the cello. The cello part is dominated by repetitive passages in which the use of natural harmonics creates a secondary rhythmic pattern. The third movement, *Energico*, brings about the conflict between the two very different "worlds" presented in the two first movements. It is aggressive, until the orderly and energetic gestures gradually find a way to coexist. The electronics cannot be separated from the instrumental in *Près;* in Karttunen's words, "they both feed one another, creating a new kind of chamber music."[49]

As a composition student in Helsinki, Saariaho was unhappy with the concert room acoustics where her early works were performed. She found that contemporary music is often played in rooms that do not have much natural resonance—in other words, acoustically "dry" places. That was her primary motivation for using amplification, which eventually led her to create soundscapes[50] of her own. In Saariaho's early works, space was often created on the multi-track tape-part of the work, from which the sounds were sent to different loudspeakers in the concert room. Today, the placing and moving of sounds in the room, in other words, the spatialization of the sounds, is calculated and controlled by computers. Selected sounds can be placed into the space (near, far away, to the right, above, etc.) as well as moved in space (away, toward, to the left, etc.); the sounds to be placed may be from the disk or captured by the microphones during the performance. The first work in which Saariaho used a special spatialization program, developed by Benedict Maillard (GRM), was *Jardin secret II* (1984–86).

Today, the spatialization of sounds can also be recalculated and carefully programmed to fit the concert hall where the work will be performed. Computers also provide the means by which virtual spaces can be created. This kind of sound-space was created for *Lonh* (1996) with the spatialization program at IRCAM. The spatialization program sends the sounds—either prerecorded or captured from the concert—to loudspeakers, which are placed around the audience. This technique creates a changing sound space in which the listener cannot actually perceive the electronic sound coming from the loudspeakers. The space of the sound can be varied and selected sounds can also be moved within this soundscape. These kinds of spatial solutions are also deployed, for instance, in *NoaNoa* (1992).

The relationship between time and space is one of the factors Saariaho has thoroughly explored. The simultaneous presence of spatial and linear aspects of music creates interesting temporal processes involving both static and progressing aspects. For instance, *La Dame à la Licorne* (1993) rings as a virtual soundscapes into which listeners are guided by the linear gestures of music.

The soundscapes created by Saariaho are imaginary virtual sounding places, which often have concrete sound elements—such as bird song, bells, and crickets—but which do not refer to any particular scenery. In musicologist Taina

Viljanen's opinion, they are "ambiguous sonoric places;" for instance, in the ballet *Maa*, summer birds are singing while the listener hears footsteps in snow.[51] The listener may recognize the sound of a bell; in actuality, it may be a synthetic sound constructed by Saariaho. She is, of course, aware of the cultural meanings of certain sounds but these meanings are not operative in her composition process; her aims are purely aesthetic. She uses recorded concrete sounds in a similar fashion, such as the use of her own footsteps on different kinds of stairs and bird song in the ballet *Maa* or the sounds of a typewriter and train in the radiophonic work *Stilleben*. The use of concrete sounds naturally originates from the ideas introduced by musique concrète.

In the 1980s, Saariaho explored the capacity of space to be one of the central parameters of a composition. Today, she no longer believes in space as a supporting musical parameter. Nevertheless, the spatialization of sound, both electronically as well as concretely, is still a central element of her work. For instance, in her first opera she placed the male and female choirs on the opposite sides of the opera hall; in the first production of her second opera, the choir's singing was electronically transmitted from another room and sent from various loudspeakers in the opera hall. In this way, the choirs contributed to the impression of a kind of socio-cultural soundscape for the events of the opera.

In the 1990s, Saariaho increased her use of live electronics as an organic part of her compositions. Nevertheless, she still works more on her sound material in non-real time, because it allows a higher quality of sound material and so she can be more certain of the result. She expands and modifies instrumental and/or human sounds in the performance using the same techniques—reverberation, harmonizing, filtering, and amplifying—as she uses when synthesizing prerecorded sounds.

Saariaho has also been innovative in refining ways of modifying sounds during a performance. For instance, in *Nuits adieux* (1991) each singer has two microphones and the voice from the hand-held microphone is set to reverb, which is controlled by the amplitude of the voice; with a soft voice, the reverb is made longer. In *Amers* (1992), as in *Près*, each string of the cello was originally amplified separately and sent to four different loudspeakers. This microphone setup, developed at IRCAM, proved very unstable and difficult to control; therefore, Saariaho later prepared new versions of both pieces without the special microphone.

Thanks to digital development, Saariaho no longer composes tape parts for her works. Tape limits the freedom of the musician to interpret the piece; the musician has to play in exact accordance with the tempo determined by the tape. Instead, she prepares the electronic files to hardware, direct on disk. She also avoids including much rhythmic material in the electronic parts in order to keep the electronics as flexible for the performer as possible. She compiles sound files on hard disk, dividing them into small segments, each of which is started by the musician using a foot pedal linked to the computer. For instance, in *Lonh* (1996) and in many other solo works, the instrumentalist or the singer controls the beginnings of different sound sequences in the work. In this way, Saariaho allows some temporal freedom, "time to breathe," for the musician.[52] Flexibility when using the electronic files is particularly important because the sound acts differently in different spaces. The acoustics of concert rooms vary; in some concert halls musical acts require much more time than in others.

Saariaho composes the electronic parts of her works by thinking of the acoustic result. She wants the musicians to focus on playing together with the electronic part in the moment, just like in a chamber music performance. The electronic dimensions of Saariaho's music reorder the conventional sounding hierarchies of music, which requires a special kind of awareness from the musician. For instance, amplification in Saariaho's music does not mean that the performer can forget the nuances of the performance and leave such matters to the sound technician. Quite the opposite. When soft sounds are amplified so that they become central in the listening experience, the musician has to be sensitive to his or her performance in a new way.

Even though the musicians can, with the foot pedal, determine the beginning of electronic sequences, the pre-programmed sound files control the temporal dimension of the performance to some extent. In all other respects the electronic sound is just a sound among others in the flow of the performance, over which the performers also can exercise control. Karttunen, for instance, experiences the part of the electronics of these sound sequences as another instrument to which he reacts like to another living musician. On the other hand, with live electronics—when electronics are used to manipulate the sounds of the cello—he regards the electronics as an extension of his cello.

The person who takes care of the electronics in the performance situation, the sound technician, is as important for the final result as the musician. Saariaho usually mixes—does the balancing, processing, and timing of the sounds—in performance, if she is present. For instance, she did the demanding mixing for the premier of her second opera together with two sound technicians. The interaction between the sound technician and the musician has to flow like the interaction between musicians in an ensemble. However, the sound technician has the power to alter the character of the acoustically played sounds by the other musicians. The supportive visual skeleton, the score, does not play a similar role in the "established order" in this kind of performance, which has to be built on the ear. Each concert hall is unique and the mixing has to be adjusted to suit the space.

Today, Saariaho usually works in her home studio, where she uses a Macintosh computer with ProTools sound editing system, samplers, programs developed at IRCAM, such as Chant, AudioSculpt, Pathwork, Max, OpenMusic, and Modalys, as well as commercial programs. Despite the new possibilities provided by technological development, Saariaho's reasons for using electronics have remained the same: to extend the musical expression of live performers, to add space and sound colors, and to create both additional and accompanying textures for the music.

Thus, Saariaho is a composer who constantly seeks new ways of integrating electronically produced sounds into the orchestral and instrumental texture. A listener can most often recognize which sounds are natural instrumental or vocal sounds—or simulations of them—and which are electronically synthesized or modified sounds; however, one can also just enjoy the varying sound qualities without trying to figure out their origin. Whether a sound originates from electronic sources or a live musician is not central for responding to Saariaho's music. In her musical vocabulary all kinds of sounds, regardless of their source of origin, are equally valuable.

4 Sounds

SAARIHO IS "A PRODUCT" of a musical world that is pluralistic without dominating musical styles or commonly shared aesthetics. Today, it is quite common for composers to explore different musical styles and composition techniques without rigidly staying within one style; even a single work may find connections with several traditions. Musical influences from different styles, past and present, and from a range of cultures open up unlimited possibilities for the composer. Saariaho's path has also passed through several compositional schools. She received a solid education in several composition techniques regarding both tonal and atonal music, both serialism and spectralism. Saariaho's production cannot be placed within a single school or musical style, and she has avoided becoming attached to any particular school of composition. She finds such labels restrictive, although she does not object when others try to label her. "I don't think much of my relationship with musical traditions. It is obvious that I come from the tradition of Western art music. I have no reason to fight against the tradition."[1]

If loosely categorized, Saariaho's works move within those streams of contemporary music that make music "for the ears," focus on sound quality, employ both electronic and acoustic means of expanding music, and renew musical conventions without opposing them. These streams of contemporary music reflect the ideas outlined by early futurists, impressionists, and expressionists and, more recently, by spectral composers. In the spirit of the spectral school, her music celebrates sound and sound colors as sources of harmony, the core of orchestration, and musical structure. Saariaho has a background in Central European avant-garde. The influence of serialism on her first composition can be witnessed in her way of organizing musical material. Her studies at IRCAM have, in their turn, left their imprints on her musical thinking, particularly with regard to her development of harmony and orchestration.

Saariaho would never simply adopt others' styles. "For me all kinds of quotations [from others' works] are completely impossible. I live and I hear and I see what's around me. [But] it must be my music. It's hard to explain, but there's something quasi-religious about my attitude to music: it must be purely what I believe in—it comes as it is and I cannot choose it."[2]

Despite numerous significant changes and developments in Saariaho's compositional style, certain features characterize her whole production. Rich timbral nuances, focused musical material evolving into unique musical forms, as well as works that call for careful listening remain her musical finger prints. Saariaho's music does not obey the rules of conventional analytical tools, since these were developed for music with distinct phrases, endings, and melodic, rhythmic, and thematic moves. Instead, it reorganizes the conventional hierarchies of musical parameters, and finds new musical forms within traditional frameworks. She finds the material for her music from computer analyses of recorded natural, instrumental, or vocal sound. Lively, vibrating sound is at the core of all the levels of her musical structure. Instrumentally or electronically varied sound color is also a form-giving principle within her music. "My music does not necessarily lead to developmental progression in the same sense that it would in romantic music, although my music does have a sense of direction which is created by using unconventional methods. The musical dynamics arise from the directions which can be heard, so that the audience perceives the direction in which music is moving."[3]

Saariaho finds inspiration in literature, film, and the visual arts, albeit staying mainly within highbrow culture. Her production mainly relates to French and Finnish cultures, although some traces of great Asian traditions can also be recognized in some pieces. When settling down in Paris, Saariaho listened to Asian music, particularly Indian classical music; she became familiar with uninterrupted, large musical forms, nuanced vocal variations, and new kinds of rhythmic structures. She felt that her musical thinking was enlarged by these listening experiences. Japanese aesthetics can most obviously be heard in *Six Japanese Gardens* (1993/1995), but it can also be sensed in the refined nuances of her flute music and in the *koto*-like sonorities of *Neiges* (1998). The Asian flavor in her music is so minor, however, that Saariaho cannot be meaningfully classified among those contemporary composers who actively draw impulses from non-Western sources.

When the music journalist Robert Maycock sought words to describe Saariaho's music in 1989, he ended up listing "exploration, introspection, beauty, pain and sensuality,"[4] hoping that these words would point to the area of feeling that is revealed to the ear. He found that "the music makes itself perfectly clear, but its sense of time and logic is remote from conceptual thinking, and it doesn't sound like anybody else's. It is liberated from the tyranny of metre and motive, yet it organises its infinitely spacious visions in concise pieces of ten or fifteen minutes."[5] In Karttunen's opinion, "Kaija's music is actually not music at all. It is pure emotion which takes the form of music. It is Kaija who writes the music, but it feels as if these works have always existed. Her music, such as *L'amour de loin*, deals with very primary situations but they are full of events in the inner sense. Underneath the surface which may seem to be treacherous calm there is the world of boiling emotions."[6] The conductor Kent Nagano regards Saariaho's music as fundamentally impressionistic. "It creates impressions of colors, impressions of pictures, and impressions of several different emotions, of a rich spirituality."[7]

Saariaho aims at writing music that is best perceived by the ear, utterly unlike what she calls "paper music"; [m]y interest is in audible structures."[8] She values musical structures that can be perceived just by hearing even though she—like any other composer— also may employ structures that may not be heard. She also emphasizes the importance of the experience over the intellect. "Sometimes the overemphasis put on the intellect irritates me, as if it would be more significant than other experiences, ways of life, and expression. In musical circles, there are many people who greatly value complex scores, although they are nothing in themselves; all that matters is whether the music touches us and on what level."[9]

Saariaho's music forces the listener to listen to music outside conventional tonality; it is music that is abstract but clear. It also requires a certain kind of musicianship and interpretation. Karttunen has observed how Saariaho's "music requires [from the musician] an interpretation that is made by the ear not by the eye—you cannot trust that the score will reveal everything about this music, because now we are dealing with such musical features that cannot be comprehended without listening to them."[10]

Saariaho's works build on unique forms, on the interplay of time and space, on the processes of tension and release, and, since the mid-1990s, on musical gestures and memory. She seeks new timbres as well as musical uses of noise.[11] In her music, the harshness of noise, however, becomes beautiful; "she reveals the beauty in sounds formerly considered noise," states Karttunen.[12] In this respect, her music can be understood as a response to the call of Luigi Russolo, a prominent painter of the Italian futurist movement of the early twentieth century, whose manifesto to futurist composers was "to continue to enlarge and enrich the field of sound."[13] He encouraged composers to "break out of this limited circle of sounds [produced by orchestral instruments] and conquer the infinite variety of noise-sounds" and to explore "the subtle and delicate noises that produce pleasing sensations."[14] In his opinion, the energetic and noisy soundscapes of modern life seek musical counterpoints that are dissonant, strange, and harsh to the ear.[15]

When noise is included as an equal, independent element within the flow of the musical progression, the conventional aesthetics of sound are expanded and the listener's ears are opened to the beauty of the noise. In Karttunen's opinion, Saariaho "gets sounds out of the cello and other instruments that were not accepted before. She surprises us, transforms our conceptions of particular sounds. She looks for beauty in absolutely everything."[16]

Among the composers who have been important to Saariaho are Bach, Sibelius, Stravinsky, Debussy, Ravel, Ligeti, and Messiaen.[17] In addition to the polyphonic structures of her music, Bach may also have inspired the polyrhythmic and polysonoric features of Saariaho's music. She claims to be nothing but honored when her music—like that of many other Finnish composers—is compared to that of Sibelius. The fifth and seventh symphonies of Sibelius as well as some his songs, for instance, *Flickan kom från sin älsklings möte*, have been her particular favorites. It is, however, difficult to find any connections between Sibelius's and Saariaho's production, other than possibly leaning toward tone poems and their use of Finnish nature as a source of inspiration. If they were not from same country, they would probably not be compared at all. Saariaho also mentions Erik Bergman (1911–2006) as an important modernist and idol for her generation of Finnish composers.

During her years as a composition student, works by Grisey and Murail—both of whom studied with Messiaen—inspired her. György Ligeti's (1923–2006) sounding masses, the scores of Luciano Berio (1925–2003), and string music by Iannis Xenakis (1922–2001) also proffered important information about composition techniques. Saariaho feels close to the Polish composer Karol Szymanowski (1882–1937), particularly his second violin concerto, and to Olivier Messiaen (1908–92), whose music also examines sound colors and the relationship between music and time. She admires Igor Stravinsky (1882–1971), who constantly renewed his musical expression, finding his own character within different kinds of musical styles despite many personal hardships. One of the most profound impressionists,

Maurice Ravel (1875–1937), was also an influential composer for a while; however, Bach is the only composer who has consistently remained a favorite.

Unsurprisingly, in France Saariaho's music is usually compared with Ravel's, who also became recognized for his refined use of sound color and instrumentation. Saariaho's piano parts particularly bring Ravel to mind. The transitions of massive orchestral and/or electronic textures as cornerstones of musical development in her works of the 1980s are reminiscent of the textures of Ligeti in the 1960s, although Saariaho's textures usually interact in a multilayered way, forming some kind of "bi- or polytexturalism."[18] Saariaho's nuanced use of instrumental techniques and musical forms echoes some works of Murail, and her capacious works of the late 1990s are distantly reminiscent of music by Toru Takemitsu (1930–96). Like Saariaho, Takemitsu also took musical impulses from paintings and nature and Messiaen was keen on bird song, which he incorporated into his musical material; for instance, Messiaen's *Saint-François d'Assise*—which was to provide a final push to Saariaho's first opera—includes possibly all the bird calls he ever noted. Karttunen also finds connections between Saariaho's music and that of Arnold Schoenberg (1874–1951), Anton Webern (1883–1945), and Alban Berg (1885–1935), three of the first European modernists of the early twentieth century. "They come from a strong romantic tradition, but they develop very personal languages. Their emotional world is so strong that nothing can hinder it from getting into their music, whatever musical language they use. This is an important parallel with Kaija's music."[19]

In addition to the previously mentioned aspects of Saariaho's music—her background in Central European avant-garde, spectralism, and serialism, the futuristic and impressionistic overtones of her music, her synesthesic imagination, and her aim to write "music for the ears"—there are five more features of her music that have, in one way or another, remained central to her musical thinking. These are the central role of timbre; the extensions of the instrumental and vocal expression; the particularization of musical form; the extreme intensity of her music; and expansions of musical conventions. They are worthy of more careful examination.

Colors and Extensions

All kinds of sounds are potential material for Saariaho's works. "The sounds of nature, all around us, are really for me the most beautiful sounds you can hear. I feel no separation between our breathing, the wind, the sea, the birds, and some of my own music. It's for me a natural continuity."[20] The world of sound is extremely rich, but conventional Western theories of music reduce the sounds to notes, which consist solely of pitch and duration and which are hierarchically ordered into octaves, the intervals of which the half-step is the smallest possible. In reality, each sound is a dynamic, constantly changing combination of sub-sounds, including a variety of microintervals, which ring as overtones of the sound. The color of sound is an intermediary of several conventional paradigms of music: pitch, tempo, rhythm, instrumentation, and harmony. They all influence our perception of sound color, which is an aspect that cannot be nailed down or fixed in any way; it lives and moves within these other parameters. In the musical works that depart from the Western theories based on the diatonic scale and tonality and are constituted around sound color, paradigms such as harmony and counterpoint either lose or change their meaning.[21]

An early work, . . . *sah den Vögeln* (Saw the Bird; 1981) for soprano, flute, oboe, cello, and prepared piano offers an illuminating example of Saariaho's sonorically rich music, which she has developed and polished greatly in her later production. It was her first work in which sound colors and the spatial impression were created electronically. It also includes unusual playing techniques for the flute and cello, which are also a characteristic feature of Saariaho's later production. The flute part includes heavy breathings, airy blows, and speaking into the instrument, as well as flute harmonics; the cello constantly changes between *sul tasto* (bowing above the fingerboard) and *sul ponticello* (bowing on or close to the bridge), and the bowing is performed with both overpressure and extremely light pressure. The sounding ideal for the prepared piano is hollow, and the soprano whispers, recites, and breathes loudly while singing.

When sounds are not defined according to their pitch and duration, they can be categorized according to other aspects, such as the slowness or the speed of the attack (the beginning of the sound) and the sound color. When these aspects are taken into account, all kinds of sounds—instrumental and concrete natural sounds, as well as synthetic and processed sounds—can be included within the same system.

During the first half of 1980s, when Saariaho studied sound synthesis and analysis, she developed her own terminology to describe the characteristics of sound color, built on dichotomies between "pure, bright sounds" and "noise," as well as "grainy, rough sounds" and "smooth sounds."[22] Organizing sounds into a continuum between sound and noise has been fairly common in electronic music since the early works by Karl-Heinz Stockhausen (1928–2007), but Saariaho's terminology also includes unusual tactile characterizations of the sounds. Smooth and bright sounds are sounds that have a harmonic overtone structure, whereas noise and rough sounds have disharmonic overtones and cannot be perceived as a distinct pitch. In Saariaho's categorization, noisy sound can be, for instance, "wind, an unpitched blow into flute, a whisper, sounds of breathing, white noise, and string instruments played *sul ponticello* or with overpressure of the bow, and so on—independent of their origin or the way they are produced—it is my way of sensing the sounds."[23] The examples she gives of the bright, pure sounds are "the harmonic sounds of string instruments, bird song, high metal percussion, the piccolo. In principle, they are of the same sort of sound material. The texture of pure sound is often smooth and it has a clear pitch identity, whereas its opposite, noisy sound, is multilayered and rough."[24] The dichotomy between noisy and bright textures enables Saariaho to construct works that relate timbre and texture with harmony. She uses the oppositional sound characters as a means of creating tension and release, comparable to harmonic progression in tonal music.

With the aid of musicians, Saariaho has examined angles such as the sounding nuances created by different playing and vocal techniques. Her computer analyses of different sonorities of acoustic instruments, voice, and various kinds of concrete sounds have further revealed the hidden dimensions of sounds. By these means she has been able to determine how the qualities of sound color can be mathematically defined and, consequently, programmed by computers. She has examined the nuances, sonority, and harmony of the sound color in order to find ways of combining the traditional notational system with sound synthesis. In addition, she has collaborated with the cognitive scientist Stephen McAdams on a study of how sound color can be a form-giving element from both the psychoacoustical and compositional perspectives.[25] She learned that because the human perception is selective, some musical parameters always dominate, and she became more attentive to the rules of human perception while composing.

Sound color operates on several levels of Saariaho's works: it acts as a form-giving principle; it provides material for the harmony of the work; and, in addition, it is also an element that lives strongly within the moment, drawing the attention of both the listener and the musician to the present moment. Instead of playing "only" notes, the musician has to produce—often by various playing techniques—vividly sounding events. A special challenge is born when the whole orchestra or different instrumental groups are used to create fields of sound color. In Salonen's experience[26] Saariaho's works challenge orchestral musicians both mentally and physically. He refers to this as a "zen challenge" because the musicians may have to maintain the same "slow motion" intensity and atmosphere for long periods of time. When conducting Saariaho's orchestral works, the main task of the conductor is to maintain the organic motion and the sense of continuity in the harmonic rather than static musical texture. Salonen stresses, however, that this is generally regarded as being one of the greatest challenges in music-making, regardless of whether one is conducting Brahms, Sibelius, or Saariaho.

Even though Saariaho has developed a rather detailed means of writing down how sound qualities can be realized by traditional instruments, no formal notational system has been developed that can enable the composer to transmit the qualities of sound in the way that the ordinary notation does for pitches and harmonies. In the actual performance situation, the precise control of timbre that Saariaho builds into her compositions becomes an aspect that has to be reacted to in performance. She also allows the musician the same space for reacting within a moment in regard to tempo: she hardly ever gives exact tempo markings. Her advice for sound technicians also encourages interpretation, because the amount of amplification, reverberation, and harmonization is indicated in percentages.

As a composer who extends our Western conceptualization of music, Saariaho has also actively sought out ways to expand the sonoric range of the human voice and traditional instruments, particularly the flute and cello, her favorite instruments. Already as a child, she was interested in blending different kinds of sounds; she sang so close to the microphone that it recorded her breathing mixed with singing. The flute is an important instrument for her because of its proximity to breathing and voice, and she regards the cello as expressing her ideas regarding sound color better than any other instrument.

Saariaho's relationship with musical traditions can also be characterized as expansive; it is as though she were constantly asking how sounds could be rethought, reorganized, sung, or played differently. However, she does not forget the musician's role in executing the music. "When I write, I always imagine the instruments very physically. If it's a cello or flute, I imagine the fingering—even with the voice, one must imagine it. It comes from the body."[27] New sound qualities never appear in Saariaho's works just for novelty's sake or a peculiar effect. She finds it interesting to seek out new sounding potentials for the voice, flute, and cello. "The main thing is to find richness of expression. In my music, that means having an abundant palette of color."[28]

The cello was one of the instruments deployed in Saariaho's earliest compositions. With the help of Anssi Karttunen, Saariaho studied the different playing techniques of the cello and their influence on the overtone structure of the sound (Photo 4). The cello has a vast register, ranging over five octaves from the low C-string to its highest harmonics. In the composer's opinion, of all the string instruments, the cello has the greatest control of the color aspects of sound. Variations of the sound color are also clearly audible. The different positions and pressures of the bow affect the overtones, which feed Saariaho's ideas about sound colors well. She creates passages that vary from noisy to clear textures; the cello produces noise when the bow is pressed hard against the strings. The left hand of the cellist also contributes to sound color in the form of various kinds of glissandos, trills, vibratos, and harmonics. Collaborating with Saariaho was also rewarding for Karttunen, who discovered new aesthetic dimensions as an instrumentalist. "I realized quite quickly that it was not a question of destroying beauty which could, indeed, be the first conclusion because our entire education as instrumentalists focuses on teaching us to control qualities of beauty in the sound to the very extreme. Now there is a composer who insists that you begin to break down this control, [which produces] the beautiful sound. And suddenly, we find new values of beauty in this deformed [broken] sound."[29]

A typical feature of Saariaho's cello sound, which can also be heard in ensemble and orchestral works as well as in the solo pieces, is the breaking of the sound by using overpressure close to the bridge, which changes the sound to rough noise. The point at which the cello sound becomes noise depends on how far the bow is from the bridge, on the speed of the bowing, and on how much pressure the player puts on the bow.

In the free-pulsative *Petals* (1988) for cello, lingering sound transformations, including trills, tremolos, vibratos, and gently echoing microtonal harmonics, develop gradually into rough textures that then withdraw back to the tiniest details of sound. The work balances on the fine line between pure sounds and deformed,

Photo 4. Anssi Karttunen and Kaija Saariaho (Helsinki, 1994). Photo courtesy of Jean-Baptiste Barrière.

 broken sounds. Different kinds of bowing techniques play a central role in the work; the new use of the bow creates a special sound world. *Petals* can be played with or without electronics. When the electronics are added, the piece gains more nuances, volume, and expression. It is clear that the broken cello sounds, amplified soft sounds, reverberation, and harmonization all determine the musical whole.

In *Spins and Spells* (1996) Saariaho developed the sound character of the cello further by using the *scordatura*, which changes the tuning of the strings from the usual and, consequently, alters the structure of the available natural harmonics and the color of the whole instrument. A particular effect, used already in the pair of orchestral works *Du cristal* and . . . *à la Fumée* (1989–90), is a trill produced by varying the pressure of the finger on the string, creating a movement between the normal pitch and a natural harmonic pitch. *Spins and Spells* is also a microscopic examination of the sonorities of the instrument, this time without electronics. It gives more time and space for the sound events than *Petals;* it lingers in varied sonorities of slowed-down sections, occasionally bursting into aggressive and rhythmic passages. In the composer's mind, these "spinning tops" and "spells" represent changes and timeless moments, respectively.

Since the qualities of the sound cannot be completely controlled by even the most careful notation, Saariaho has to take the whole scale of possible musical events into account when composing. This is why Karttunen regards her music as "elastic." Due to its processual, escaping nature, he feels unable to completely control the flow of music; instead, the musical process with all its little differences and accidents controls the musician. The performer has to internalize a new way of musical thinking, which demands surrendering himself or herself to the flow of small nuances and powerful noise sounds. Karttunen says that Saariaho's works teach the musician a new kind of sensitivity; participating in the moment also strongly affects the audience. "The contact between the audience, the music, and the performer is exceptionally strong. Afterward hardly anybody comes to speak about not understanding the music because it deals with such fundamental and basic emotions."[30] Karttunen also thanks Saariaho for expanding the range of the cello. "The cello is much richer, in a technical sense, thanks to Kaija. Her studies on the different aspects of sound and that she breaks the borders [of conventional cello sound] by adding bow pressure [to the strings] is no longer an accident but an intended sound event. Simultaneously, the sound expands in many different dimensions, from the dark to the bright. This is an organic part of Kaija's world when to many other composers it is just an effect. Kaija has transformed the effect into [musical] grammar."[31]

The point at which breathing evolves into a sound is Saariaho's central fascination in the sound of the flute; "in my mind, the flute relates to breathing, it is an enlargement of breathing."[32] She is interested in the ritualistic history of the flute, which is an archaic instrument. She regards the flute as an intimate instrument particularly because of the presence of breathing. Her writing for the flute includes various kinds of "breathy sounds" and combines various playing techniques; she regulates blowing and varies the sounds produced by the flutist through special trills, tremolos, multiphonics, glissando, and Flatterzunge (flutter tonguing)—to spoken, whispered, and sung words, sentences, and phonemes.[33] The listener hears various kinds of transitions, from short glides and glissandos to longer continuums between breathing, whispering, and pure flute sounds. In addition, Saariaho utilizes electronics as an expansion of the flute sound. In many works, such as in *Laconisme de l'aile*, *NoaNoa*, and her flute concerto *Aile du Songe*, voice and instrumental sounds blend together when the flutist recites or whispers words while playing.

The flute sound is conventionally regarded as creating breathy "aeolian" sounds only by mistake. Breaking the conventionally beautiful flute sound with breathy sounds and flutter tonguing, key clicks, and varied vibratos began already in the early 1900s.[34] Spoken words became a frequent feature of flute music much later, in the 1970s. Among many others, Saariaho's teacher from Freiburg Musikhochschule, Brian Ferneyhough, utilizes breathings and speech in his works for flute. Unlike Saariaho, however, he tends to restrict, diminish, or in some other way control the breathing of the flutist.[35]

The characteristics of Saariaho's writing for the flute can be heard in her early works *. . . sah den Vögeln* (1981) and *Laconisme de l'aile* (1982). Both of them build on tensions created by contrasting bright sounds and noise. In the latter work, written in Freiburg, sounds produced by whispering and speaking as well as different kinds of playing techniques fluidly evolve into an organic whole. Her study companion in Freiburg, the flutist Anne Eirola (née Rautio) to whom the work is dedicated, uses words such as *intense*, *mystic*, *hypnotic*, *sensitive*, *beautiful*, and *fragile* to describe its special atmosphere.[36] The work begins with a stanza from a poem written by the Nobel Prize winner Saint-John Perse (1887–1975), recited by the flutist while blowing the flute. "Ignorant of their shadow, knowing of death only that immortal part which is consumed in the distant glamour of great waters, they pass and leave us and we are no longer the same. They are space traversed by a single thought."[37] In Saariaho's interpretation, the poet writes about the flight of the birds metaphorically to describe mysteries of life. Interestingly, Perse's poem is a reflection on paintings done by Georges Braque, witnessing possibly similar kinds of "cross-artistic" sensations as Saariaho has with her music. The reciting develops, without a break, into a pure flute sound, which varies from one sound quality and playing technique to another, from airy whistles to "pure" sounds, from playing into singing and whispers, from whispers to whistle sounds, and so on, occasionally spiced with key clicks and flutter tonguing. The melodic line mainly progresses in upward and downward glissandos—they can also be played as scales—in wide leaps and microintervals. The work ends with soft and gentle overtones, produced by carefully controlled blowing. Saariaho was inspired by the themes of the poems of Saint-Perse, the metaphorical representations of the birds and the sea. In Saariaho's mind, the abstract sound quality of the flute is well suited for representing birds; the flute draws the abstract flight paths of the birds.[38] Hoitenga, who has often performed *Laconisme de l'aile*, perceives on her part the birds as representing the desire to ascend to a higher sphere.

Saariaho has collaborated with many flutists, but primarily with Hoitenga, to whom she has dedicated many works for the flute. In all, Saariaho has composed five works for solo flute and one flute concerto, but the flute has an important role in many of her other works as well. In the solo work *NoaNoa* (1992) and in the flute concerto *Aile du Songe* (2001), she utilizes sonoric and melodic ideas for the flute, for which she has, together with Hoitenga, sought out "flutist-friendly" solutions. *NoaNoa* for solo flute and electronics includes several sequences in which whispers and instrumental sounds blend together; its prerecorded electronic sounds also include whispers, creating the impression of intimacy and secrecy.[39]

Saariaho's style of writing for the flute allows space for breathing and for the individual tempi and interpretation of the instrumentalist. In Hoitenga's opinion, she has "a very clear idea of the range of sounds a flute can produce—ranging from archaic breath-sounds to more lyrical, traditionally refined flute sounds."[40] Hoitenga also draws connections between the intimate use of breath in Saariaho's flute works and the Japanese shakuhachi bamboo flute tradition in which "the preparation for producing the sound is the most important aspect, while the Western concept is that the sound is everything and it does not matter how you achieve it."[41] Shakuhachi aesthetics also includes a variety of breathy sounds.

When composing for the flute, Saariaho thinks sensitively of the instrument and the flutist's way of producing sounds, allowing the musician to create an organic way of playing. According to Hoitenga, Saariaho's works for the flute explore "flexibility within the range of possibility," examining its sound world from "its archaic origins to its most refined ways of expression." Flute parts written by Saariaho do not present "a polished conservatory sound," but they breathe, whisper, and speak, reflecting humanness in all its aspects. Since Saariaho's way of notating her music for the flute includes so much information about dynamics, character, and playing techniques, musicians may have difficulty noticing how much interpretative freedom they have. As in her cello compositions, electronics in the works for the flute extend the instrument and provide more dimensions to the instrumental sound. Interesting polyphonic textures evolve when the sound of the flute is reverberated and the player continues to play.

Carefully notated whispering with rhythmic and articulation advice is a recurrent sound quality not only in Saariaho's works for flute but also in other instrumental works; for instance, in *Jardin secret II* for cembalo and tape, *Lichtbogen*, *Nymphea*, and . . . *à la Fumée* the amplified whispers blend into the instrumental texture. Even though the musicians whisper words or sentences, their meanings cannot be fully grasped; the sounds of whispering become music in themselves. The whispered texts, however, always have a deeper implication for the work. For instance, in *Nymphea* (1987) for string quartet the musicians whisper lines written by Arseniy Tarkovsky, father of the film director Andrei Tarkovsky: "The summer is gone, and might never have been. In the sunshine it's warm, but there has to be more. It all came to pass, all fell into my hands like a five-petalled leaf. But there has to be more."[42] The whispers are wired up to a delay program, which mystifies them further. Again, the recited poem cannot be comprehended but Saariaho wished to include it in the work anyway; she used the whispered sounds to create a part of the musical texture.

The new playing techniques and unconventional hierarchy of musical parameters included in Saariaho's music challenge performers who are used to conventional art music to find new ways to use their bodies. Speaking, breathing, and whispering are intimate acts that demand a new performance attitude from the flutist, who has been taught to hide the effort made to produce a sound.[43] The flutist has to learn how to speak while blowing into the flute. For most flutists, simultaneously speaking and playing is difficult at first. It requires an expanded awareness and new ways of using mouth muscles. The electronic parts on the hard disk that are controlled by the player with the pedal also challenge the coordination of the flutist. In the orchestral and chamber music works including amplification of soft sounds, the musician has to play carefully even the softest sounds in order to produce the desired sound quality. Saariaho does not use amplification to even out problems of balance, but, instead, to pick up sound characters that otherwise could not be heard. The breaking of sound may also be difficult for a performer who is trained to produce conventionally beautiful sounds.

The alternations between noise and bright sound that are so typical of Saariaho's works for flute and cello find their counterpart in her vocal production, which has undergone significant changes over the years. The human voice and breathing evolving into speaking or singing have fascinated Saariaho since her childhood. As a composer she has sought the intimacy and immediacy of vocal expression also by investigating other alternative dimensions of singing, such as the details of pronunciation and the possibilities provided by amplification. She has aimed at writing vocal music nearer to the intimate human voice, whispers, and speech as well as "the 'voice' of our thinking."[44]

Although Saariaho's first compositions were vocal works, it took a long time before she felt that she had found her own way of writing for the voice. Her early vocal works, *. . . sah den Vögeln*, *Preludi-Tunnustus-Postludi* (text from the Bible), *Du gick, flög* (You Went, Flew; to the text by Gunnar Björling) and *Adjö* (Farewell; to the text of Solveig von Schultz), all from 1981–82, were not followed until 1988, when two larger vocal compositions *From the Grammar of Dreams* (to the text of Sylvia Plath) and *Grammaire des rêves* (to the text of Paul Eluard) were premiered. Even though the names of these works are reminiscent of each other, they are musically very different; the former study emotional states produced by different vocal techniques, whereas in the latter, the vocal lines blend into the instrumental texture in chamber music manner.

The range of vocal expression from whispers to singing in the high register, which is a typical feature of Saariaho's vocal works, is also related to her categorization of sounds from noise to bright colors. *Grammaire des rêves* (1988) as well as *Nuits, adieux* (Nights, Farewells; 1991) are good examples of her style of writing vocal music, which moves between breathings, whispers, and singing. The text for *Nuits, adieux* originates in Jacques Roubaud's *Échange de la lumière* (Exchange of Thoughts about Light) in which people speak about light. *Nuits, adieux* is the culmination of Saariaho's exactness of writing for the extreme aspects of the voice. Each singer has two microphones, one for recording sounds for endless reverberation—which Saariaho regards as the metaphor for memory—and another for voices in linear progression. Interestingly, this kind of singing style, including deep sighs and heavy breathing, is reminiscent of the ancient lamenting tradition of Karelia, the original homeland of Saariaho's grandmother, to whom this "lullaby" is dedicated.

Saariaho has felt that the classical bel canto singing style is too abstract and distant from her experiences of voice, although she always takes into account the singers' training based on the bel canto tradition. For instance, in *Caliban's Dream* (1993) and *Miranda's Lament* (1997), both written to the text of William Shakespeare, she encourages the singer to strive for a natural style of vocal production. Saariaho is fascinated by the way the voice shares many characteristics with musical instruments, and how it can be blended into the overall orchestral sound. In several works, various forms of voice formation often appear as one of the instruments, blending into the orchestral or ensemble sound.

After *Nuits, adieux,* Saariaho simplified her vocal notation, although fluid continuations between speech, sighs, and song still play a role in her vocal music. The frequency of vocal works increased since the mid-1990s, when she began to develop ideas for an opera. Since then, her vocal works have been more melodic. The five-movement *Château de l'âme* (1995) for solo soprano, eight female voices, and orchestra is her first vocal work to include an orchestra. The impressionistic colors of the orchestration and female voices closely follow with the strong emotional expressions written for the solo voice. *Die Aussicht* (The View; 1996) is a short and airy melodic study for soprano, flute, violin, cello, and guitar to the text of Friedrich Hölderlin. *Lonh* (From Afar; 1996) for soprano and electronics is a lingering tone poem that consists of a (at times electronically processed) sensual and expressive vocal melodic line that moves in a refined, electronically created virtual soundscape. The soundscape includes, in addition to electronic sounds, sounds of wind, birds, and rain. The traces of speech intonation so typical of Saariaho's earlier vocal works have in these works of late 1990s diminished into short glides, vibratos, and occasional spoken words.

To date, Saariaho's output for the voice comprises of some thirty works, most of them for soprano voice, which she regards as her "own voice, a woman's voice."[45] Some of her works, such as *Caliban's Dream* and *Prospero's Vision,* as well as her operas, include male roles. In typical Saariaho style, the composer has dedicated much time to studying the details of voice formation from the perspective of the performer, particularly those that relate to the pronunciation of vowels and consonants. "Nowadays, I am very aware of the location of different phonemes in the singer's head and throat and I avoid using certain vowels in certain registers. As far as singing is concerned, I actually have begun to think in a similar, physical or bodily way as I think of other instruments."[46]

In 2002, Saariaho completed the dramatically varying song cycle *Quatre instants* for soprano and piano (an alternative version has also been composed for orchestra) for the Finnish-born, world-renowned soprano Karita Mattila (b. 1960).[47] Mattila praises Saariaho's dedication to musicians. "There hardly is another composer like she. When Kaija was composing *Quatre instants* for me, she traveled to listen to me in different [solo] tasks. The work suits my voice well although it is a demanding work to sing."[48]

Processes and Expansions

A listener who is only familiar with conventional uses of sound color will certainly have her or his musical perceptions enlarged by the experience of attending a performance of Saariaho's works. The listeners sensitized to Western conventions cannot anticipate the progression of Saariaho's pieces in their normal ways because the musical progression often builds on changes in the sound color. Moreover, the idiosyncratic forms of Saariaho's works, the extreme intensity invested in every musical moment, as well as the skillful "temporal play" between static spatiality and forward-moving gestures in them challenge both listeners and performers to live in the moment. These features make us experience her music with a particular sensibility that grows out of the performance itself.

In Saariaho's opinion, traditional musical forms lack the capacity to surprise today's listener. "We easily become bored by the traditional forms because we know all too well how the work proceeds. If you want to make personal music, you have to deal with the form anew."[49] Citing Kandinsky, Saariaho regards the form as an external manifestation of internal meaning;[50] in her works, the form is always found in close relation to her musical material. In her mind, form and musical material are inseparable.

Whereas classical musical dramaturgy is based on the building up and resolving of a climax, Saariaho's futuristic spirit has led her to question this form and develop alternative solutions.[51] For instance, *Verblendungen* (1982–84) opposes the traditional musical form that gradually develops toward a climax; it begins with a grand climax, and proceeds by building multidimensional transformations between different kinds of musical material during the course of which the climax of the beginning is gradually resolved.

In Western tonal musical thinking, the building up and resolving of tensions mainly takes place through harmonic tonal functions, consonances, and dissonances. Spectral composers were searching for ways to create tensions with timbral changes,[52] outside tonal thinking. Saariaho began to deploy sound color as one of the building blocks of form already in her early works, for instance, in *Im Träume* (In Dream; 1980) for cello and piano, the harmony is stable while sudden changes characterize the texture and tone color. "It can be said that these two elements [sound color and harmony] become confused when timbre becomes an integral part of form and when harmony, by contrast, is confined to determining the general sonority."[53] Somewhat later, she began to create tensions with the help of timbral dichotomies. In her music, sonority and dynamics are used in a manner similar to that of harmonic tonal functions in more conventional music; directional musical processes are constructed between different kinds of distinct, oppositional musical characters. As explained earlier, she deploys the oppositional sound colors, "bright" and noisy sounds, as well as "grainy" and "smooth" sounds, to build directional transitions and movements, as well as tensions and releases. For instance, in *Lichtbogen* (1985–86), noise develops into a pure sound, which then gradually returns to noise. When these kinds of opposing forces meet, interesting tensional states are born.

The idea of idiosyncratic global forms built on sonoric changes is connected to the French spectral school. However, as Stoianova has stated, Saariaho's music—unlike that of most spectral composers—has a strong sense of temporal proportions; "like living organisms the musical structure [in Saariaho's music] oscillates between two concepts, on the one hand, repetition and regularity, on the other hand, variability and complexity, hence the rhythm comes an active dimension of the language."[54]

Since Saariaho defines the form and material individually for each work, the formal structures of her works are diverse. Some characteristic formal solutions can, however, be noted. The most usual form in Saariaho's works of the 1980s is a slow transition between different kinds of musical characters. An illustrative example of a work with such a transitional form is *Vers le blanc* (1982), which includes a slow glide from one chord to another over a period of fifteen minutes. During these fifteen minutes, the conventional hierarchy between harmony and timbre is reversed. The time-related and rhythmic aspects seem to be marginal in comparison with the massive sound textures. Many of Saariaho's works from the 1980s evolve through similar slow processes, which give the first impression of rhythmically rather uneventful slow music. Even though the temporality of her music seems to be replaced by slowly transforming sounding textures, this is not the complete story. Beneath this surface there are rapid musical events and the listener's first impression proves false when the musical texture is more carefully examined. For instance, when the rhythm is intensified into a trill or tremolo, it loses its rhythmic character and will only be perceived as a sound color. Similarly, harmonic changes may also be perceived being merely changes in sound color.

Thus, Saariaho's music moves rhythmically on many different levels. The oppositional, even conflicting simultaneous rhythms are also interesting. For instance, in *Amers* (1992) Stoianova identified linear, polyphonic, and homophonic methods of managing time.[55] Simultaneous, overlapping, and sometimes contradicting processes on different musical levels characterize Saariaho's music. Due to these numerous, simultaneous processes, nothing in the music can be reduced to a single event. This gives the strong impression of an ever-changing, inevitable flow of events—thereby, metaphorically representing the nature of life.

In her multi-channel works, such as *Jardin secret I* (1984–85) for tape and *Jardin secret II* (1984–86) for harpsichord and tape, Saariaho experimented with space as the important factor in the pieces' musical progression. Thanks to four-channel tape recorders and, later, spatialization programs, she could place selected sounds into the space as well as move within it. Although these experiments made Saariaho skeptical about spatiality as a form-giving musical dimension,[56] her interest in creating virtual spaces through sounds has not withered. Many of her works, such as the tape installation *La Dame à la Licorne* (1993) and *Lonh* (1996), can be experienced as sounding spaces that seem to exist in their own right. When the work begins, the listener is allowed to enter this musical space, and the space remains even after the listener has departed. This impression is strengthened by the gradual beginnings and faded endings of these works. The titles of her works, such as *Jardin secret* (Secret Garden), *Six Japanese Gardens*, and those that refer to the cosmos (*Orion*, *Solar*, and *Lichtbogen* [Arches of Light]), strengthen these spatial associations.

In works composed during the latter part of the 1980s, including *Jardin secret I*, the overall form may be based on two distinctly different rhythmic characters, which possibly echoes Kandinsky's theory according to which the form is perceived through contradictions and negations. Or, they even may have their roots in Saariaho's school years: "When composing, I often draw sketches of form about the musical events moving in time. Formal structures often aim at either creating symmetry and/or breaking it down. In both cases, the awareness of symmetry is present in my works. The extent to which this awareness and the need to build and/or to destroy the symmetry is based on the form drawing exercises I did as a child remains unknown to me. What I know about the work of other composers, however, points to the possibility that this axis in my work is more important than is generally the case."[57]

The two parts of the string quartet *Nymphea* (1987) have distinct characters; according to the composer, "bright and fragile textures" meet with "violent, fragmenting masses of sound."[58] In both *Amers* (1992) and the violin concerto *Graal théâtre* (1994), the first part presents the musical material and the second part plays more freely and more dramatically with the same material. The musicologist Kimmo Korhonen has noted that the musical content in *Graal théâtre* reflects the introverted and sacred character of the "grail" and the theatrical and extrovert nature of the "theatre."[59] The form may also be built on rhythmic oppositions; for instance, the middle parts of *Neiges* (1998) for eight cellos, which has been described by the composer as "a set of variations on snow," have a regular pulse whereas the first and the last parts are merely studies of the sound color, without a pulse.

In Saariaho's works, the oppositions do not seem to be competing about the victory like the theme and the sub-theme in a classical symphony. Instead, when they meet, they jointly create a new sonic space, a new state of mind, without creating a fusion. The last part of the work may, thereby, become a meeting of two opposites that do not compete or lose their individual identities.

Melody has gradually gained more significance in Saariaho's works since the early 1990s. In the early works, such as in *Im Träume* (1980) for cello and piano, there were short melodic sequences consisting of large intervals. Later, short melodic bursts were included in solo works and works for solistic instruments, such as in the violin concerto *Graal théâtre* (1994), in which Saariaho studied the relationship between the melodic line and harmony. In the orchestral work *Du cristal* (1989–90) melodies are played in unison by piano, harp, and mallet instruments. The melodies in all these works have a fragmented, unfinished character and often their capacity to maintain a recognizable identity is tested against changes in sound color and tempo. The melodic way of writing was further developed in the works Saariaho wrote for voice in the late 1990s, when she was preparing to write an opera; *Château de l'âme* (1995) and *Lonh* (1996) include emotionally charged, soaring melodies.

As the melodic thinking grew stronger in Saariaho's works, her use of rhythm also gained new aspects. One of the first signs was the perceivable, physical pulse of the heart beats included in *Du cristal.* From there on, it is as if the bodily side of rhythm and music had entered into Saariaho's musical thinking. She contrasts two different ways to build time: music without a pulse, in which the sense of time is lost and music becomes space; and music with a pulse, which is reminiscent of a heartbeat. "For me, all the expressive dimensions of music can be placed between these two, opposite musical characters, the first reaching our imagination and mind, the second touching us physically on a more primitive level. The absence of a physical beat leaves space for more refined and deeper aspects of musical language."[60] The change in Saariaho's rhythmical thinking over the course of the 1990s can be observed when comparing, for instance, the cello works *Petals* (1988) with *Sept papillons* (2000): *Petals* is a free-pulsative work, whereas in the miniatures of *Sept papillons,* the seven different representations of butterflies can be heard as rhythmic studies.

The first movement, "L'oiseau dansant" (Dancing Bird), of the second part of *Aile du songe* (Wing of Dream; 2001) evidenced the arrival of a more playful and, in Saariaho's words, "primitive" rhythm in her music. By "primitive rhythm," Saariaho refers to bodily rhythms, rhythms that entice one to dance. The focal point for the flute concerto was an aboriginal tale about a dancing bird, and Saariaho was seeking a musical expression for joy that would also honor the energetic character of Camilla Hoitenga, to whom the work is dedicated. Although an active rhythm was motivated by these aspects, composing rhythmically active music did not come naturally to Saariaho. She had to make herself to compose it. The poetry about birds, "Oiseaux" by Saint-John Perse, which inspired Saariaho to compose her early work for the flute, *Laconisme de l'aile* (1982), was also one of the inspirations for *Aile du Songe.*

A characteristic feature of Saariaho's works of the late 1990s and early 2000s is her use of reoccurring musical gestures—in other words, recognizable, distinct combinations of melodic, rhythmic, sonoric qualities—which call for the listener's memory. Each of the opera characters in *L' amour de loin*, as well as in *Adriana Mater*, have their characteristic musical gestures, which consist of a combination of melodic lines, rhythms, and instrumentations. Even though the musical gestures are constantly varied, they provide consistency. They are like people: they gather new experiences and remember the past differently than before; nevertheless, they maintain their recognizable identity.

Saariaho's latest works draw widely on her previous musical explorations. She continues to create sound color through variety of media, including electronics. Sound color in her newer works is also created through orchestration and accurately defined singing and playing techniques. For instance, in *Oltra mar* (1999) for choir and orchestra (the theme of which is voyage—one of the central themes of *L' amour de loin*) the choir creates essential aspects of color. She still deploys electronics, usually in the form of spatialization and live electronics, albeit less frequently than in her younger years. For instance, her basic idea when composing *Nymphea Reflections* (2001) for strings was to write to the strings the sound colors that had been created in *Nymphea* (1987) by live electronics. The same can be clearly heard also in her later works, such as in the cello concerto *Notes of Light* (2007). Her recent works are also based on idiosyncratic forms that arise from the musical material, and vice versa. Saariaho may also draw from musical transitions. For instance, the first part of the orchestral work *Orion* (2002) with its large sound textures is reminiscent of earlier orchestral works, *Du cristal* and *. . . à la Fumée* (1989–90). The two other parts present the newer emphases in Saariaho's music: distinct melodic lines on the surface of spacious backgrounds and clear rhythmic pulsations.

5 Dramas

DESPITE SAARIAHO'S PROTESTATIONS in the 1980s that she would never write an opera, and even though some music critics were surprised when she did produce such works, her operatic works can also be understood as a logical continuation of her development as a composer. Opera combines several art forms and Saariaho's musical path has always moved fluidly over their meeting points. She has had a special interest in the human voice in its various forms since childhood, and vocal works written to carefully chosen literary texts have been an important facet of her production since her early years as a composer. The themes of the texts she has chosen to compose have been those of great dramas concerning the ambiguous nature of love and life. Her understanding of the nature of sound, its color and spatiality applied to voice, instruments, instrumentation, and orchestration, as well as her works building on long-lasting arcs of tension on many levels of the musical texture, have also paved the way toward her creation of intensive large-scale dramas.

Writing an opera was a natural result of Saariaho's musical creativity, which draws from multisensory sensations. The visual dimension of her musical imagination and her tendency to become musically inspired by literary texts provided fruitful ground for the creation of staged art. Some of her earlier works have also been visualized, for instance, *The Grammar of Dreams* (a collection of seven works from 1986 to 2000) was staged with lighting and costumes.

Opera is also a natural art form for a composer who likes to collaborate and who is able to create functional and inspirational working relationships with other people. In addition to being keen on collaborating with trusted musicians, Saariaho has over the years worked with several sound technicians, painters, dancers, and filmmakers. Even though most of the collaboration regarding an opera production takes place after the work has been composed, it is crucial for the present-day composer to find such collaborators who will support her or his musical ideas.

It took years for Saariaho to be able to identify her own relationship with the operatic tradition. Some of her early plans for multimedia works functioned as the first steps toward operatic thinking, but the idea of writing an opera only became logical to her when she felt the need to write music for a story line that would require remaining within a certain theme for a long time. She began to plan an opera in the early 1990s, after having completed the ballet *Maa.* Love and death, the most typical themes of the opera tradition, fascinated her, and she wanted to approach them through her compositions. She was also interested in spiritual opera.

Opera is a meeting point of music, literature, theater and other visual arts, staging, and lighting. It is also a product of collaboration between people who have backgrounds in different arts and, thus, multiple viewpoints. This "democratic principle of opera," as Peter Sellars calls it, requires a shared space and the kind of collaboration where "there is not enough room for disagreement without weakening the whole, but at the same time everything becomes stronger—when the opera is done, it is a very rich texture with layers of series of experiences that has almost the same kind of layering as life has"[1] (Photo 5). Sellars describes how this layering of events creates the magic of the opera: "Human beings need permission—and that's metaphor—to recognize that there are many layers of reality moving at any given moment, and that every small gesture has very large consequences. So opera is this amazing form, which takes a gesture, and understands it through music, poetry, dance, visual art, all at the same time."

Musically, Saariaho's first opera, *L'amour de loin*, builds on the central features of her idiom: it celebrates sound color through rich orchestration, by electronic means, as well as by expanded vocal and instrumental techniques. Sellars, who is used to creating the staging on the basis of the orchestral score, soon discovered that Saariaho's music, where "every little movement in the spiritual consciousness is printed with high intensity,"[2] requires a different kind of working method. "With Kaija's music, the things you expect to hear when reading the score, you

Photo 5. A long-term collaborator, conductor Esa-Pekka Salonen, Kaija Saariaho, and Peter Sellars at the national premiere of L'amour de loin *at the Finnish National Opera House (Helsinki, 2000). Photo courtesy of Leif Weckström.*

do not hear. It is so mysterious, it does not sound as it looks like on the page, it goes into another sound world."

Saariaho did not develop and experiment with her new musical ideas in smaller works before beginning to compose her second opera. With *Adriana Mater* (2006), she moved directly toward more dramatic writing, an operatic tragedy, which examines its characters—a mother, her sister and her rapist, the father of her unborn son—during a war. The theme of the opera arose over a dinner with Maalouf after they had seen a performance concerning motherhood that had upset Saariaho with its stereotypical solutions. As a mother, Saariaho wanted to bring a woman's perspective to the events of war. Maalouf, on his part, had experienced war when working as a war reporter. Sellars was also part of the team from the very beginning of the working process. In his opinion, *Adriana Mater* addresses important moral concerns in a deeply emotional way. "When Kaija takes on a subject that is here and now, a day-to-day world that is confronting us every moment, her musical representation of that dramatizes it so deeply, all these levels of hurt, invisible wounds and invisible states. In fact, life is a series of deep emotions and soul states that are moving our lives every minute. The zone of feeling that we pass through in our lives is a place that most of us are not very articulate about and do not really recognize in our lives. Kaija's music seizes from that place."

The Saariaho-Maalouf-Sellars team does not fear making art that awakens emotions and touches the divine. In that respect, Saariaho's music differs greatly from the music of the previous generation of European serialism, which valued the abstract musical structures produced by a detached and supposedly objective frame of mind. Roughly stated, in those contexts music that evoked emotions and was appreciated by the listeners was dismissed as bad music. Saariaho's music opposes such values and so Sellars finds a depth of feeling that corresponds to "our search for a language that can express an emotion that saturates the time we are living in but that is strangely unacknowledged." He appreciates the detailed sensibility of Saariaho's music. "[I]t is highly theatrical in the sense that it dramatizes the life of the soul, it dramatizes this inner movement, leaving most of the events of the outer world apart."

Operas

L'amour de loin is an opera lasting about two hours divided into five scenes and thirteen acts. The main roles are sung by a soprano, a baritone, and a mezzo soprano who sings a male role, thus, a so-called travesty role. The composition also involves a male and female choir, which does not necessarily sing on the stage with the soloists; in Sellars's production, the choir is placed on opposite balconies on either side of the stage. The orchestra is enlarged with extra percussionists and a keyboard player who produces the electronics, controlled by sound technicians.

The plot of *L'amour de loin* originates in the life story and distant love of a twelfth-century troubadour, Jaufré Rudel. The original stanzas from his life story, the *vida*, are the basis for the opera libretto, and Jaufré's special song composed by Saariaho has some influences from the original fragmental notation. The opera recounts the story of two ill-fated lovers, the prince and troubadour from Blaye (near Bordeaux, in present-day France), Jaufré, and the Countess of Tripoli (in present-day Lebanon), Clémence. The third character is a pilgrim, who travels and mediates between these two. The troubadour is tired of his present life of entertainments. When visiting Blaye, the pilgrim tells him about the Countess who lives in Tripoli and Jaufré falls in love with her although he has never seen her. He composes songs describing his distant love. When the pilgrim visits Tripoli again, he sings one of Jaufré's songs to her, also describing the troubadour who sings about her. At first, Clémence doubts whether she is worthy of his love, but eventually she falls in love with her distant admirer. Jaufré and the pilgrim take a journey across the sea toward Tripoli to meet the Countess. On the voyage, Jaufré falls ill and dreams about their meeting. When they arrive in Tripoli and the couple finally meets, he dies in her arms. At first, the Countess curses her fate, but gradually her grief transforms into acceptance and love.

The libretto works on several levels: it provides the basic plot of the drama, its settings and scenes, and the poetic dialogues reveal the nature of the main characters, their thoughts and mental states. Jaufré and Clémence are unruly nobles whose longing for something other than their current lives leads them to transformational events, whereas the androgynous character of the pilgrim is a mediator and messenger between the couple and their two worlds, Orient and Occident. His unfortunate role is to function as an innocent messenger of death. They are all strangers in their surroundings: Jaufré among his friends, Clémence in her present home in a foreign country, and the pilgrim everywhere on his pilgrimage. From the point of its characters, the opera is Clémence's story: she is the seeker and questioner who, in the course of the events and through intensive emotions and grief, develops from being a vain young woman to being capable of mature love and, finally, of attaining enlightenment. Jaufré, despite his courage to begin his journey to meet his love, remains the victim of his fate, whereas the pilgrim in his stability gives the impression of coming from another, timeless world.

While Saariaho was writing the opera, its characters began to live in her mind. This experience is common among authors. The story became her story. "Later I understood that the story concerns me personally. There are these two main characters—the troubadour who wants to express his love through writing music, and the lady who was sent to a foreign continent. I realized that they are like the two parts of myself."[3] Saariaho regards this story of love, longing, distance, and dreams as being accurate about today's world as well; the lovers create illusions about one another but are afraid of confronting reality. When hearing about Jaufré's love and longing, Clémence suffers from great doubt. Jaufré's fate is to die at the moment when his dreams and wishes are about to become true because, ultimately, he lacked the strength to face reality.

The libretto has been influenced by several different traditions. Musicologist Liisamaija Hautsalo regards it as an inter-text between the Christian Crusades made during the twelfth century, the troubadour tradition, Persian love poetry, biblical texts, and the opera tradition.[4] She interprets the opera as an allegory of the search for the transcendent: the theme of longing for a distant love can also be understood as a longing for the divine. In the Persian tradition, mysticism and love poetry fuse and the object of desire may be seen both as the divine being and as an earthly beloved. Hautsalo interprets, in biblical terms, the pilgrim as an angel, Jaufré's journey as *via doloroso,* and Clémence as a symbol of mercy and as a gate through which Jaufré moves toward resurrection.[5] However, for Saariaho, the opera does not have any biblical dimensions. Although Hautsalo may overemphasize the biblical features of the opera characters, they certainly evoke multiple associations. The opera rises above the mundane and an ordinary love story. The spiritual dimension is particularly plausible in the last act, in which Clémence prays: "If your name is Love, I worship you, Lord; If your name is Goodness, I worship you; If your name is forgiveness, I worship you, Lord; If your name is Suffering, I worship you." However, we do not know whether Clémence is singing to her lost lover or to God. At the end of the opera, when Clémence grieves for the loss of her beloved one, Jaufré, the music follows in real time, moving with her changing emotional states. According to Saariaho,[6] Clémence ("mercy" in French) understands that death does not end loving, whereas in Sellars's interpretation, Clémence is moving toward spiritual enlightenment. According to the score, the music of this last act changes "into air and light."

The music of the opera reminds listeners of both the Orient and the medieval era, without compromising Saariaho's idiom. The influences from early periods of music history are few and distant; they are most obvious in the sonoric qualities created by perfect fifths and fourths played on the harps and in the melody sung by the baritone, which is slightly influenced by the fragmental original notation of *Languan li jorn*, a stanza by Jaufré Rudel. This melody is first sung in French by the pilgrim when he tells Clémence about Jaufré. The same song is later heard twice, sung in Occitanian by Clémence. The poem encapsulates the theme of the opera, longing for a distant love.[7] The use of Occitanian increases the medieval atmosphere. The Oriental flavor, for its part, arises from microtonality and melismatic vocal lines. The medieval and Oriental flavors of *L'amour de loin* blend fluidly into the extremely rich sonoric landscape that moves the lyrical, albeit tragic story forward. Even though the music sometimes hints at distant places and far-off times, the holistic impression is of a kind of contemporary music that comes so close to the listener that she or he recognizes the emotional moves and inner processes represented through the music as though they were her or his own.

The main characters of *L'amour de loin* are emphasized with certain musical gestures, specific harmonic structures, and instrumentations: Jaufré's music includes perfect fourths and fifths played in arpeggio by harps and in the spirit of troubadour songs; his vocal parts move stepwise within a narrow register. Clémence's music is characterized by rising scales and wide leaps within a large ambitus, accompanied by fifths played by the harps. Rich ornamentations and short glissandis of her vocal line create an Oriental atmosphere. The pilgrim's presence is announced by descending scales, played in turns by piccolo and three other flutes.[8]

The orchestra comprises thirty different kinds of instruments to produce an exceptionally large variation of colors within constantly changing, shimmering sound fields; the harmonic structures are often so thick that they appear as sound color. The sonority is further enriched by an innovative use of instrumental sections, for example, the first violin section is divided into four different groups or the same melodic line is played one after another by different instruments. Orchestral colors are also created by unconventional playing techniques. The enlarged section of percussions and electronics, which melt into the instrumental and vocal textures, add their own flavor to the rich sonority. The Renaissance-sounding *borduna* sounds, harps, as well as allusions to medieval modality and troubadour ballads as well as reminiscences of Japanese timbres are smoothly integrated into Saariaho's orchestral texture and melodic formations.

The consonant musical language combines impressionistic features with spectralism. The vocal lines and orchestration jointly form a constantly glacially moving organism: the ever-changing colors created by the orchestration merely reflect and interact in chamber music style with the vocal lines instead of simply accompanying them. The vocal lines are firmly foregrounded; they are never overshadowed by the orchestral texture.

The music follows the thoughts and emotions of the main characters with great intensity. Peter Sellars regards the music "as almost private. It is a world where every heartbeat and every movement of the heart means something—it is like a seismograph—every little movement in the spiritual awareness set onto paper with great intensity—is carefully examined."[9] The male and female choruses—representing Jaufré' s male companions and Clémence's female Tripolean friends who comment upon the events and advise the main characters—enlarge the orchestral sound with human compassion. The choruses are also used to create soundscapes, such as the wavelike sounds of the sea. In the last act their song is reminiscent of a hymn, which stresses Clémence's spiritual transcendence.

The drama begins with three acts that present the main characters musically through chanting, with sparse orchestral means.[10] As the story deepens to explore the main themes of the opera, love and longing, the musical texture becomes more dense. The third act includes more dramatic, emotional events. The song of the pilgrim in the third act, which essentializes the theme of the opera, is emphasized with clearer musical gestures, creating a sense of timelessness. The fourth act is the journey across the sea, during which Jaufré falls ill and dreams of Clémence. He regrets taking the journey; "from afar, the sun is the light of heaven but from closer it is fire of the hell." His fear is stressed by massive sound fields; the sounding capacity of the orchestra and the choirs is used to maximum effect. The journey across the sea can be interpreted as a transformation from merely dreaming and longing to reality. In the final, fifth act, the musical tension is gradually released and the texture becomes thinner. After Jaufré has died, grieving "we do not earn love, we betray love," Clémence rages and curses her fate and God and the music regains its stunning power. The hymn accompanies her turning toward divine love. Toward the end, the orchestra ceases and the electronics fill in the soundspace until they, too, vanish into the air.

The opera builds on several binaries: it is about the encounter of pair of ill-fated lovers, a man and a woman who seek their way between worldly and divine love. It is about the meeting between East and West, Orient and Occident. Geographically, it takes place in two locations, in South France and Lebanon, "green grass and trees versus stones," and the plot moves between the land and the sea, "spices, flowers, smells and heath versus the sea and humidity."[11] Musically, it combines the romantic opera tradition with contemporary spectral aesthetics and medieval modality. According to musicologist Sanna Iitti, the opera expands the pairs of opposites that characterize Saariaho's musical thinking to encompass and represent human psychological tensions arising from the conflict between desire and fear.[12]

The opera's thematic content—love, longing, and death—marks *L'amour de loin* as belonging to the romantic opera tradition. The theme of *L'amour de loin* is reminiscent of Wagner's *Tristan and Isolde:* they both have a rather simple plot, which emphasizes the development of the main characters. They are about ill-fated love that ends with the death of the main character; both Jaufré and Tristan are knights who die of an illness caused by their longing and suffering. Jaufré's existential journey results in greater understanding of life and Tristan also ends his life in an increased state of spiritual enlightenment. Unsurprisingly, *L'amour de loin* and *Tristan and Isolde* do not have anything musical in common; they are products of vastly different stylistic periods in Western art music. As an operatic whole, *L'amour loin* is most closely related to the European tradition of spiritual opera, in which its counterparts are Messiaen's *St.François d'Assise* and Claude Debussy's *Pelleas and Melisande.* In regard to the events on the stage, they are rather static dramas, which create mystical atmospheres and follow the changes of the inner mental states of their characters intensively. The impressionistic dimensions of Saariaho's music relate to that of Debussy and his *Pelleas and Melisande.* Both Messiaen and Saariaho are difficult composers to categorize; they share the same respect for sound color, large sound fields, and airiness of musical texture, as well as the inward intensity of the moment. *St. François d'Assise* impresses the listener with its thick sound fields and large performing machinery; thus, Messiaen's massive musical epics contrast with Saariaho's lyrical and tender music, although both are emotionally powerful music.

Whereas *L'amour de loin* drew on the entire range of musical paths Saariaho took since the early 1980s, her second opera, *Adriana Mater* (2006), added a new, dramatic, and epic expression to her musical vocabulary. Although it is also clearly a product of Saariaho's idiom, it is utterly unlike the lyrical and airy *L' amour de loin;* the overall impression is of dark, rough music while the subject matter is heavy and violent: "The orchestration is more impatient, more dramatic than in my earlier works. It's a single dark color, with two pianos[13] to provide the necessary sharp attack and definition."[14] The orchestra of over eighty musicians is dominated by full sets of percussions played by five percussionists, and further enhanced by the two grand pianos. In addition to the standard sound sources of Saariaho's idiom—strings creating sound fields, harps, flutes, and bells—the brass and woodwinds have important roles to play. The choir functions as part of the orchestra and is not necessarily seen by the audience; in the first production of the opera, it sang in a separate room and the sounds were transferred to the audience by an electronic surround system. The choir takes on the role of commentator; as a kind of character's inner voice it shouts and whispers but rarely sings texts in an ordinary way. Electronics—sound processing and circulation, reverberation and amplification—are used in a refined way; they melt fluidly into the whole.

The libretto of *Adriana Mater*, written by Amin Maalouf, examines the cruelties caused by the war in one village and their tragic consequences in the villagers' lives. The dominant perspective is that of a woman and mother who agonizes over the character of her growing son. Both Saariaho and Maalouf wished to write an opera that would comment on current issues. "It's important to create characters who really speak to us, and speak about important things."[15] They did not want to create stereotypical pictures of good people and bad people. "We all have so many sides of ourselves. I would like to see the complexity of our relationships."[16]

The characters in the opera are Adriana and her sister Refka, Adriana's rapist Tsargo, and Yonas, a son who is born as a consequence of the rape. The events of the opera take place before the war, during the war, and seventeen years thereafter. The place and time are undefined; the same tragedy could have happened long ago or today.

The story begins when Adriana refuses the drunken Tsargo. Tsargo feels humiliated and vows to take revenge. During the war, he returns to his home village as a soldier. When he is again refused by Adriana, he rapes her. Adriana becomes pregnant and she decides to keep the child. Together with her sister Refka, she agonizes over whether the unborn child will be like Cain or Abel. When the son, Yonas, finds out at the age of seventeen that his father is a rapist and not a war hero as he has been told, he confronts his mother. When he hears that Tsargo has returned to the village, he leaves to seek out his monster father. Adriana tries to prevent him, but he swears to kill Tsargo. Adriana must leave the fatal decision to her son; "if he must kill him, he kills him." Yonas finds his father blind, ruined by the war. He flees without being able to take revenge and goes to apologize his mother. Adriana, however, is relieved. She feels that Yonas is of her blood, not of his father's; "we did not avenge but we were redeemed."

Churning sound fields and continuums dominate the musical texture, which is dramatized by rhythmic and sonoric means. The music creates the war and follows the tragedy of its victims. Its intensity is stressed by the economical, focused musical material. The solo parts move on the extremes of their register, exploiting their potentials to the full. The prose text written by Maalouf led Saariaho to write monosyllabic vocal lines without decorations. Only the dream scenes, which were added to the libretto at Saariaho's behest, include melismatic vocal lines. Electronic sound processing is also used within the dream scenes. During the second and last dream scene, the opera rises to its climax.

The emotional states of the characters are stressed by means of rhythmically accented orchestration that often moves in the lower registers and in fortissimo; Saariaho's sounds "live" emphatically together with the characters, with their longing, hate, pride, despair, fear, and search for consolation. As in *L'amour de loin*, each character has his or her own musical material, whether it is harmonic, modal, or rhythmic motifs that are varied during the course of the performance: Adriana and Refka are linked with particular modes; their duets are the most beautiful parts of the opera. Adriana is characterized by the low strings and soft sonority, whereas Tsargo is shadowed by bassoons. The connectedness between Adriana and her son, Yonas, is stressed by "the heart motif"—simultaneously fast and slower pulsating tempos that appeared for the first time in *Du cristal* (1989–90). The heart motif appears first when Adriana is pregnant and again whenever the mother and the son meet; the simultaneous pulsations symbolize their relationship.[17]

Despite its dramatic events, such as the rape, the focus of *Adriana Mater* lies in the inner thoughts and mental development of its characters. The inner evolution of the characters is reflected through their respective musical gestures, which are reduced toward the end. In this respect, *Adriana Mater* is like *L'amour de loin*. Certain thematic oppositions can also be identified: motherhood is contrasted with war, home with an enemy.

Saariaho regards *Adriana Mater* as a parable of our time. It presents the horrors of war in the mirror of maternity: despite the war, which causes passion to become rape and integrity to fall into ruins, humanity, motherhood, and love are preserved. The enemy is not a stranger; the librettist Maalouf did not want to give the impression that all evil comes from "the other."[18] Sellars's staging in Opera Bastille added a dimension of hope that was not included in Maalouf's libretto: in the final scene, Yonas and Adriana make emphatic gestures toward blind Tsargo. Through Sellars's interpretation, the opera asks whether the circle of violence, hatred, revenge, and killing can be stopped by forgiveness. The tragedy seeks consolation from forgiveness; this interpretation is supported by the music, which calms down in clear harmony of thirds toward the end, although neither Saariaho nor Maalouf thought of the theme of forgiveness when writing the opera.[19]

Passions

Saariaho finished *Adriana Mater* on Sunday, and on the following Saturday, she began to work on *La Passion de Simone* (2006), an oratorio for solo soprano, choir, orchestra, and electronics. She was eager to begin to compose a work about Simone Weil (1909–43), the French-Jewish philosopher and mystic. The choices Weil made during her own life—to work as a teacher, a factory worker, a member of the French resistance (without arms), and, finally, to starve to death when refusing to eat more than people got to eat in the concentration camps—witnessed the key conviction of her philosophy: our obligation to respect and love "the other."

Saariaho's first contact with Weil's texts was at the age of seventeen, when she read *Gravity and Grace* (1947), a book compiled by Weil's friend Gustave Thibon from her notebooks after her death. In these notes, Weil contrasts the gravity of the mundane world with the liberating power of grace. Thibon encapsulates her words as a message to the humankind, eternally "enslaved by gravity and liberated by grace."[20] For Weil, the supernatural was "the light itself"; however, she stressed that "the object of our search should not be supernatural but the world."[21] Weil's spiritual search, severe asceticism, and passionate quest for truth appealed to Saariaho. The book became so important that it moved together with her to Freiburg in 1981. Later she read Weil's writings and biographies in the original language, French, in order to learn more about her philosophy.

The idea of focusing on Simone Weil was born when Saariaho and Sellars discovered that they were both keen admirers of her writings. Their interests in and images of Weil were, however, different; Saariaho is fascinated by her striving for abstract, intellectual, and spiritual goals, whereas Sellars's interest lies in her social awareness and political activities; he praises Weil as an example of female spirituality and as a role model for the twenty-first century.[22] Maalouf's task was to bring these dimensions together, showing the fate of a frail human being in relation to these great ideas. Like Weil's philosophy, the libretto addresses many fundamental questions of human existence.

Saariaho and Maalouf jointly selected the parts of Weil's life and work to be included in the libretto. Although Saariaho wanted the text to be short, it still manages to describe Weil's sufferings and death within fifteen "stations." The text and the performance operate on three levels. On the first, direct, spoken quotations from Weil have been recorded and are played from the computer against an electronic surround. On the second, the soprano sings, telling about Weil's life. On the third, the choir comments upon her life and the choices she makes. Both the soprano and the electronic part together with the spoken voice are embedded in the sound fields created by the orchestra and the choir.

Only the outer form of *La Passion de Simone* and the sacred dimensions of Weil's sufferings relate to the tradition of oratorio; musically, it continues the path opened by Saariaho's operas: *La Passion de Simone* is sensitive and lyrical like *L'amour de loin*, but also tragic and dark like *Adriana Mater*. Its musical form is reminiscent of a large symphonic form. Saariaho wanted plentiful space for music within the complete work in order to express the spiritual essence of Weil's text and the quality of her presence. Maalouf's poetic text provided impulses for different types of vocal writings, allowing Saariaho's music space to breathe. The transparent nature of Saariaho's musical language is once again revealed in *La Passion de Simone*. The work expresses both pain and beauty, suffering and heightening—in fact, gravity and grace. In Weil's words; "Moral gravity makes us fall towards the heights."[23] Sellars claims that "very few things ever written are so intense as *La Passion de Simone*. And at the same time it is so generous, so warm, so humane and very modest—[it] opens a space where you are listening to your own heart, where you are listening deeply. For me, this is the impulse: you have to listen more deeply."[24]

This section of the chapter is not titled "Passions" solely in reference to *La Passion de Simone*, but also because it is a term that encapsulates Saariaho's relationship to music. She is a deeply dedicated composer who does not have any other alternative in her life but composing; she claims that music provides the cornerstone of her identity. Her passionate relationship with music inevitably concerns all aspects of her work as a composer: her working habits, her firm and long-lasting relationships with excellent musicians, her selection of commissions and projects, and her skill to navigate her way within the world of contemporary music, as well as with the media. The talent of perceiving sounds in encounters with the world in its visual, imaginary, and literary richness may have fallen as an inborn gift to Saariaho but everything else she has produced and achieved is a result of passionate, hard work.

Two aspects of Saariaho's character dominate the composition process: on the one hand she is a highly rational person who is obedient to Lutheran work ethics, and on the other hand, she is driven to create by the way she senses and perceives the world. The combination of these two extremes provides fruitful ground for the work, which requires both the creativity to explore new dimensions of music and the disciplined rational mind to work the ideas into intellectually sculptured musical works. The very same extremes are also the dimensions Saariaho loves most in composition work. In her opinion, composers and musicians are privileged because their work requires continuous development, which allows them to get closer and deeper into the music. "The interesting thing in our work is the possibility to learn and develop oneself as long as we live. Do we use this possibility? I see the artist as a spiritual person disturbed all the time with temptations of fame, money, easiness, and, to some extent, also technology."[25]

Saariaho works intensively, combining moments of inspiration with strict self-discipline. She forces herself to continuously seek out new expressions to be included in her musical language. "Ninety-five percent of the process of the composition work is *sisua*[26] (guts). It is slow and hard work. I love having a comfortable life, with my children and my husband. But every day I spend most of my time in my study, otherwise there would not be any music."[27] She is well organized, and this can be seen in her ordinary life as a mother and a composer.

For Saariaho, composing is a completely self-contained world. She does not consciously seek out inspiration from nature or from the other arts, although such moments occasionally happen. The best musical ideas arise from work. She compares composing with meditation, in which new information is gained quite differently from that received in the rest of one's life. This experience humbles her and leads her to believe that her music goes beyond that which is written on the paper. "I see something very spiritual in this work; we have to be really honest and really humble."[28] Saariaho has not spoken much about the spirituality of her art, but when reading the theorists and thinkers who have inspired her it becomes obvious. This leads one to consider what kind of spirituality can be related to Saariaho's work. In my understanding, her spirituality can be found in her careful and respectful craftsmanship: the strongest image of Saariaho is that of a hard-working individual who seeks the deepest truths from within herself. This interpretation has a parallel in Weil's thoughts: "Intelligence can never penetrate the mystery, but it, and it alone can judge of the suitability of the words which express it. For this task it needs to be keener, more discerning, more precise, more exact and more exacting than for any other."[29] Saariaho does not accept any dogmas because for her music is "limitless"; rather, she accepts music "as part of the mystery of the nature, close to such things as love or death. What do we finally know about those things?"[30]

Saariaho's musical language has become more concentrated in recent years: all her previous explorations of the sound and form have been necessary for the formation of her current musical style. She seems to have left out everything unnecessary in the aesthetic core of her music. Her later works present less spatiality and more linearity and recognizable melodies than before, and rhythm has become a more central aspect of her music. The intervallic and rhythmic identity of musical gestures remains recognizable, while their timbral quality may pass through several metamorphoses. Her musical expression also resembles the traditional aspects of Western art more closely now that her own musical expression is strong enough to confront these traditions as an equal. She has written compositions within the classical traditions of concert, opera, and oratorio.

Unlike many other composers, Saariaho has not abandoned electronics as merely a youthful experiment but, instead, regards electronics as a necessary tool for realizing richer sound worlds. When compared to her works of the 1980s, however, her most recent works include much less sampled sounds. In these works, electronics are usually used sparsely to process sounds in real time during the performance. For instance, *Adriana Mater* does not include electronically produced sounds from outside the score: only amplification is used and the sound space of the dream scenes is changed electronically. Many transitions, transformations, and glissandos that previously were produced electronically are now written for orchestral instruments. For instance, in the cello concerto *Notes of Light* (2007) the expansions of the sound of the cello, which were previously produced electronically, are skillfully written for orchestral instruments: the sounds of the cello are continued either by the flutes, piccolo, or violins. The original idea of the work was about "light filtering in various ways through transparent sound material."[31]

Saariaho's latest production maintains the essential characteristics of her musical style, albeit in a more fully crystallized form: sound color created through a wide variety of means—by playing techniques, orchestration, harmony, and sound technology—continues to play a crucial role in the musical texture. Her works make varied expansions of conventional musical aesthetics, for instance, noise sounds produced by various playing techniques are integrated into instrumental and/or vocal musical texture as its natural part. Her music includes different kinds of "close examinations" of sound and its harmonic structure, studying its tiniest details. She finds the form anew for each work, thus, particularization of form is still central to her composition process. Her recent musical works also maintain the importance of dichotomies, both as extreme points of small scale transitions of sound and as basic elements of formal structure.

Saariaho fulfills the fundamental ideology of new music by always searching for new solutions. She seems to have a strong, almost uncompromising will, which directs her musical path and keeps her faithful to her own musical idiom. This leads her to find her path outside the conventions of fashionable schools of music, while simultaneously building on the foundations of the existing canon. Thus, her music invests and deploys all possible means of enlivening and enriching the tradition. Saariaho's musical production questions many aspects of conventional musical thinking, either by expanding existing boundaries, for instance, witnessing of the firm formal thinking outside of conventional, given forms, or reversing the conventional hierarchy of musical paradigms, such as placing sound color over pitch and harmony. Even though she has shown greater concern for classical musical genres during the last decade and composed solo concertos—a violin concerto, a flute concerto, and a cello concerto—two operas and an oratorio, each time her works have expanded our comprehension of those musical traditions. Despite the multifaceted enlargements and expansions Saariaho's music makes on existing musical conventions, it never confronts or opposes the tradition of Western art music.

In a lecture at the University of California, San Diego, in 1999, Saariaho asked, "what kinds of impressions, thoughts and feelings are we able to leave to others with our music?"[32] On the basis of what I have learned during the course of writing this book, I would like to reply that her music encourages us to hear, look, and feel differently. It teaches us to focus on the things and events that are in-between, things that, at first, might not seem to be so important but that locate at the points where gravity is lightened by grace. It teaches us about the importance of looking for new solutions, new styles of being in the world, while learning from and respectfully acknowledging existing traditions. Her music provides a narrative of the twenty-first century, and makes us realize that, despite the great discoveries of the past and ideologies of our Western culture, we still must find new paths.

> The work of art has an author and yet, when it is perfect, it has something which is essentially anonymous about it. It imitates the anonymity of divine art. In the same way the beauty of the world proves to be a God who is personal and impersonal at the same time and is neither the one nor the other separately.[33]

NOTES

CHAPTER 1: *Biography*

1. Saariaho interview, June 13, 1988, Helsinki, Finland. The quotes in this chapter are from the same interview. Unless otherwise stated, all quoted interviews were made by the author, Pirkko Moisala.

2. Saariaho in a brochure of the Temet Company (Helsinki: Temet Company, 2002), 7.

3. The first school developed by Steiner was designed for the children of the workers of the Waldorf Astoria factory.

4. Saariaho cited in Marja Dahlström, *Muodosta minuuteen* (Helsinki: Edita, 1999), 87–88.

5. Ibid.

6. In 1973, the school was developed into the University of Industrial Arts.

7. Sibelius provided the young Finnish nation with national pride, both during the process of nation-building as well as during the years of the Second World War when his *Finlandia* was listened to as a narrative of war ending in the peace of a triumphant nation.

8. Marcia Citron, *Gender and the Musical Canon* (Cambridge: Cambridge University Press, 1993), 55–78.

9. Salonen phone interview, September 15, 2006.

10. Saariaho on the TV program *Suomalaiset sävelet 8/8*, ed. Tiina-Maija Lehtonen, Finnish Broadcasting Corporation, TV1, 2006.

11. Salonen phone interview, September 15, 2006.

12. Ibid.

13. Saariaho in *Suomalaiset sävelet*, 2006.

14. Salonen phone interview, September 15, 2006.

15. In the summer of 2006, Saariaho was the artistic director of the festival.

16. Seppo Heikinheimo, *Helsingin Sanomat* (April 10, 1983).

17. Seppo Heikinheimo, *Helsingin Sanomat* (August 11, 1990).

18. Spectral composers base the compositions on the sound spectrum. Sound spectrum is a physical concept, which refers to the components of sound frequencies, the hierarchy of sub-sounds, and their amplitudes.

19. Saariaho cited in Pierre Michel, "Entretien avec Kaija Saariaho," in *Kaija Saariaho. Compositeurs d'aujourd'hui* 6, ed. Risto Nieminen, Les cahiers de l'Ircam (Paris: IRCAM—Center Georges-Pompidou, 1994), 8.

20. Hoitenga interview, January 27, 2002, Turku, Finland.

21. Juri Reinvere, "Vastab Kaija Saariaho," *Teater-Musica-Kino* (Estonia: Tallinn, 1999), 6.

22. Saariaho cited in Cori Ellison, "Uncovering Beauty in Ordinary Noise," *The New York Times* (November 7, 1999).

23. Saariaho cited by Vesa Sirén in http://virtual.finland.fi (September 15, 2006).

24. Tristan Murail, "Spectra and Pixies" (trans. Tod Machover), *Contemporary Music Review* 1(1) (1984): 158.

25. Gérard Grisey, "Zur Entstehung des Klanges," in *Darmstädter Beiträge der Neuen Musik XVII*, Ferienkurse '78, ed. Ernst Thomas (Mainz: B. Scott's Söhne, 1978), 78–79.

26. Murail, "Spectra and Pixies," 161–63.

27. Saariaho in *The New York Times* (November 7, 1999).

28. Robert Morgan, *Twentieth-Century Music* (New York: Norton & Company, 1991), 463.

29. Saariaho in "Harvest," *Prisma* CD-ROM, *The Musical World of Kaija Saariaho* (Porvoo: WSOY, 1999).

30. Karttunen interview, November 27, 2001, Paris, France.

31. The anthropological study based on fieldwork conducted by Georgina Born: *Rationalizing Culture. IRCAM, Boulex, and the Institutionalization of the Musical Avant-Garde* (Berkeley: University of California Press, 1995), investigates IRCAM as a social institution.

32. At IRCAM, she has collaborated, among others, with Jan Vandenheeden, Ramón Gonzáles-Arroyon, and Xavier Chabot.

33. See For Further Reading.

34. Seppo Heikinheimo, *Helsingin Sanomat* (April 11, 1984).

35. Heikki Aaltoila, *Uusi Suomi* (April 13, 1984).

36. Robin Freeman, *Contact 31* (Autumn 1986).

37. Saariaho in *Helsingin Sanomat* (October 23, 1983).

38. Risto Nieminen, *Kaija Saariaho* (Helsinki: Finnish Music Information Center, 1988).

39. Heikki Aaltoila, *Uusi Suomi* (February 28, 1991).

40. Saariaho in *Uusi Suomi* (June 23, 1988).

41. Kaija Saariaho, "Matter and Mind in Music," in *Matter and Mind in Architecture*, ed. Pirkko Tuukkanen (Hämeenlinna: Karisto, 2000), 111.

42. Ibid.

43. Saariaho cited in Jodelet, Florent, "Entretien, Kaija Saariaho. The Queen of Finland . . . in Japan," from unknown publication in Saariaho's home archives, 21–24.

44. Ibid.

45. Saariaho cited by Anders Beyer, "Till Death Us Do Part. A Portrait of the Finnish Composer Kaija Saariaho," *Nordic Sounds* 1 (2008): 8–9

46. Ibid.

47. Janne, the nickname for Jean, refers to Jean Sibelius.

48. Kai Amberla, " Kaija Saariaho: Elämää musiikin kautta, musiikkia elämän kautta," *Rondo* 8 (1995): 4.

49. Saariaho in *Prisma* CD-ROM, *The Musical World of Kaija Saariaho* (Porvoo: WSOY, 1999).

50. Saariaho interview, October 6, 2006, Paris, France.

51. Saariaho interview, October 20, 2005, Vilnius, Lithuania.

52. Saariaho cited by Beyer, "Till Death Us Do Part," 9.

53. Saariaho interview, March 16, 2001, Turku, Finland.

54. Saariaho in "Harvest," *Prisma* CD-ROM, *The Musical World of Kaija Saariaho* (Helsinki: WSOY, 1999).

55. Upshaw interview, November 28, 2001, Paris, France. The other quotations from her are from the same source.

56. Saariaho cited by Cori Ellison, *New York Times* (July 21, 2002).

57. Saariaho, November 26, 2006, Kunstler Hause, Vienna, Austria.

58. Ibid.

59. Sellars in an interview, www.pbs.org/wgbh/questionofgod/voices/sellars.html, WGBH Educational Foundation (July 21, 2004).

60. Gilles Macassar, Télérama (November 21, 2001).

61. Kathy Nellens interview, November 29, 2001, Paris, France.

62. Saariaho, November 26, 2006, Künstler Hause, Vienna, Austria.

63. Saariaho interview, October 20, 2005, Vilnius, Lithuania.

64. Saariaho, "Minä, maani, maailmassa," *Arsis Bulletin* 4 (2005): 5.

65. Saariaho in *RTRS-Interview* by Michael Roddy (March 29, 2006).

66. Saariaho in *Suomalaiset sävelet*, 2006.

CHAPTER 2: *Developments*

1. Kaija Saariaho cited in Michael Kurtz, "Kaija Saariaho—silmän ja korvan välinen yhteistyö," *Takoja* 3 (2006): 11.

2. Juhani Nuorvala, *Saariaho in Profile*, 1991. www.fimic.fi (February 12, 2007).

3. Jukka Isopuro, *Helsingin Sanomat* (September 16, 1997).

4. Saariaho cited in Andrew Ford, "Bows of Light," *ABC Radio* (July 1993), 92–97.

5. Saariaho cited in *The Wire*, in 2000.

6. Saariaho cited in *The New York Times* (July 21, 2002).

7. John von Rhien, *The Chicago Tribune* (May 24, 1988).

8. Andy Hamilton, *The Wire*, date unknown, from Saariaho's home archives.

9. Lars Hedblad, *Svenska Dagbladet* (November 14, 2000).

10. The titles of Saariaho's works do not have official English translations.

11. See Kaija Saariaho, "Timbre and Harmony: Interpolations of Timbral Structures," *Contemporary Music Review* 2(1) (1987): 93–133, as well as "Vestreute Gedanken zur Komplexität in der Musik" and "Rhythmische Interpolationen," in *Klangportraits*, Band 4, ed. Susanne Winterfeldt, (Kassel: Furore Verlag. 1991), 33–35.

12. Mike Silverton, *Fanfare* (May/June 1990), 273.

13. Liimatainen interview, September 29, 2001, Helsinki, Finland. All the interviews quoted in this chapter were made by the author, Pirkko Moisala.

14. Saariaho cited in Márta Grabócz, "La musique contemporaine finlandaise: Conception gestuelle de la macrostructure. Kaija Saariaho et Magnus Lindberg," *Les Cahiers du Cirem - Musique et geste*, December 92–Mars 93, (26–27):157.

15. Alan Rich, *Los Angeles Herald Examiner*, date unknown, 1989. From Saariaho's home archives.

16. Saariaho in a concert program (Tampere: Tampere Biennale, April 5, 1998).

17. Gavin Thomas and Anthony Bye, "Northern Nights. Just How Tender is the North?" *The Musical Times* (February 1993): 100.

18. Ibid.

19. Saariaho lecture, April 1998, Sibelius Academy, Helsinki, Finland.

20. Anne Sivuoja-Gunaratnam, "Rhetoric of Transition in Kaija Saariaho's Music," in *Musical Signification: Between Rhetoric and Pragmatics. Proceedings of the 5th International Congress on Musical Signification*, ed. Gino Stefani, Eero Tarasti, and Luca Marconi (Bologna: CLUEB, 1998), 537–42.

21. Saariaho citation, ibid. She refers to *Briefe an Milena* by Franz Kafka (1952).

22. Edward Seckerson, *The Independent* (June 1993), date unknown, from Saariaho's home archives.

23. Saariaho cited in Laurence Vittes, "Cristal Quest—Philharmonic Takes Up Saariaho's Pursuit of Musical Symmetry," unknown date and newspaper, from Saariaho's home archives.

24. Salonen cited in John Henken, "Prepping for L.A.'s Podium—Fine-Tuning the Philharmonic for Salonen's '92 Takeover," unknown newspaper from Saariaho's home archives.

25. Barry Millington, *The Times* (October 13, 1994).

26. Saariaho, ibid.

27. The title comes from a book by Henri Atlan, *Entre le cristal et la fumée.*

28. Greg Hettmansberger, *The Daily News* (November 7, 1992).

29. Andrew Ford, *The Australian Financial Review* (July 5, 2002).

30. Stephen Pettitt, "First from the Finns," unknown newspaper from Saariaho's home archives.

31. Andrew Clements, *The Financial Times Weekend* (December 12–13, 1992).

32. Ivanka Stoianova, "Spectra," *Prisma* CD-ROM, *The Musical World of Kaija Saariaho* (Helsinki: WSOY, 1999).

33. Jacques Roubaud, (avec Florence Delay), *Graal théâtre* (Paris: Gallimard, 1977).

34. Anne Sivuoja-Gunaratnam has interpreted Lonh as creating "a poetic of unresolved distance" in "Desire and Distance in Kaija Saariaho's Lonh," *Organized Sound, an International Journal of Music Technology* 8(1) (2003): 71–85.

35. Richard Dyer, *The Boston Globe*, date unknown, from Saariaho's home archives.

36. Christopher Schluren, *Rondo* (6) (1996): 36.

37. Allan Kozinn, *The New York Times*, date unknown, from Saariaho's home archives.

38. Jacques Roubaud, *La fleur inverse: essai sur l'art formel des troubadours* (Ramsay, 1986).

39. Saariaho interview, March 15, 2001, Turku, Finland.

40. CD Booklet of *Private Gardens*, ODE 906–2, Ondine, 1997.

41. John Story, *Fanfare* (May/June 1998).

42. Saariaho in the concert program of the premiere given by the New York Philharmonics, which also commissioned the work.

43. David Murray, *The Financial Times (August 25, 2000).*

44. Wolfgang Sandner, *Frankfurter Allgemeine Zeitung* (August 17, 2000).

45. "[B]esticht durch ihre zarten, flimmernden, schwelenden, funkelnden, vibrierenden Klangfärben, die an den französischen Impressionismus ebenso erinnern wie an Messiaen. Auch Live-Elektronik wird verwendet—allerdings in einer sehr sparsamen Art, bei der die Technik nie im Vordergrund steht." H. G. Pribil, *Wiener Zeitung* (August 18, 2000).

46. Shirley Fleming, *Musicalamerica.com (August 21, 2000).*

47. Anthony Tommassini, *The New York Times (August 17, 2000).*

48. Anthony Tommassini, "A Haunting New Opera," *The New York Times,* (December 31, 2000).

49. Humphrey Burton, *BBC Music Magazine (December 1, 2000).*

50. Hilary Finch in *The Times* (October 30, 2001)

51. Spano cited by Craig Smith, *The New Mexican,* date unknown, from Saariaho's home archives.

52. Shirley Fleming, *MusicalAmerica.com* (July 31, 2002).

53. Cori Ellison, *The New York Times* (July 21, 2002).

54. James R. Oestreich, *The New York Times (July 30, 2002).*

55. Alex Ross, *The New Yorker* (April 24, 2006).

56. Justin Davidson at www.newsday.com (February 8, 2003).

57. Saariaho interview, October 21, 2005, Vilnius, Lithuania.

58. Tim Ashley, *The Guardian (April 7, 2003).*

59. Pierre Gervasoni, *Le Monde* (August 4, 2003).

60. Tim Page, *The Washington Post* (December 29, 2002).

61. Saariaho cited in Liisa Hautsalo, "Sliding in Sound—Material and Immaterial Images in Kaija Saariaho's Flute Music," *Finnish Music Quarterly* 1 (2003): 32.

62. John von Rhein, *The Chicago Tribune* (July 8, 2002).

63. Alan Riding, *The New York Times* (April 6, 2006).

64. Francis Carlin, *Financial Times* (April 4, 2006).

65. Olivier Olgan, *La Tribune* (April 4, 2006).

66. Jörg von Ülhermann, *Die Welt* (April 5, 2006).

67. Alex Ross, *The New Yorker* (April 24, 2006).

68. Ibid.

CHAPTER 3: *Work*

1. Saariaho cited in Michael Kurtz, "Kaija Saariaho—silmän ja korvan välinen yhteistyö," *Takoja* 3 (2006): 11.

2. Saariaho interview, July 28 1998, Helsinki, Finland. All interviews quoted in this chapter were made by the author, Pirkko Moisala.

3. Saariaho in a brochure of the Temet Company (Helsinki: Temet Company, 2002), 7.

4. Ibid.

5. Kaija Saariaho, "Matter and Mind in Music," in *Matter and Mind in Architecture*, ed. Pirkko Tuukkanen (Hämeenlinna: Karisto, 2000), 111.

6. Ibid.

7. Karttunen interview, November 27, 2001, Paris, France.

8. Saariaho cited in Jüri Reinvere, "Vastab Kaija Saariaho," *Teater-Muusika-Kino* (Estonia: Tallinn, 1999), 6.

9. Saariaho cited in Risto Nieminen, "A Portrait of Kaija Saariaho," *Nordic Sounds* (June 1986).

10. Richard E. Cytowic, *Synesthesia: A Union of the Senses.* (New York: Springer Verlag, 1989). The concept of synesthesia is built on the distinctions between sensation and perception on the one hand, and between discrete modalities on the other. This distinction has also been questioned. For instance, the philosopher Merleau-Ponty (1962), who is known as the philosopher of the body, does not regard the body as a collection of adjacent organs but as "a synergic system, all the functions which are exercised and linked together in the general action of being in the world" (ibid., 234). From this point of view, the distinction between discrete modalities, hearing and seeing, vanishes.

11. Saariaho cited in Nieminen, "A Portrait of Kaija Saariaho."

12. Saariaho in "Harvest," *Prisma* CD-ROM.

13. Saariaho cited in Kai Amberla, "Kaija Saariaho: Elämää musiikin kautta, musiikkia elämän kautta," *Rondo* 8 (1995): 7.

14. This description makes an interesting parallel to the way the fifth grade in the Waldorf school is taught about a plant, described by Saariaho's school teacher Marja Dahlström: "The plant is a mediator between the sky and the earth, light and darkness. It grows simultaneously towards the sun and down to the earth. It relates to the wholeness of its environment, to its every element: to earth, water, ear and warmth"(Marja Dahlström: *Muodosta minuuteen* [Helsinki: Edita, 1999], 23). The symmetry of natural phenomena is carefully investigated within Steiner pedagogy, which probably has strengthened Saariaho's capacity to observe forms in nature.

15. Saariaho cited in *The New York Times* (November 7, 1999).

16. Arnold Schopenhauer, *The World as Will and Representations,* trans. E. F. J. Paine. (New York: Dower, 1966), vol. 1: 262–63.

17. Saint-John Perse, whose texts have inspired several Saariaho's works, also has a poem named *Amers* (Seamarks).

18. Saariaho cited in Kimmo Korhonen, *Kaija Saariaho in Profile I* (1995/1998 www .fimic.fi).

19. Karttunen interview, November 27, 2001, Paris, France.

20. Saariaho interview, December 6, 2000, Paris, France.

21. Saariaho in *The Times* (October 30, 2001).

22. Saariaho interview, March 16, 2002, Turku, Finland.

23. In 1897–1926, Claude Monet painted more than two hundred pictures, including a gigantic series of water lilies, "pursuing his attempt to pinpoint the ephemeral appearance of things, their metamorphosis up to the point of deliquescence" (Marianne Delafond and

Caroline Genet-Bondeville: *Monet in the Time of the Water Lilies* [Paris: Èditions Scala, 2002], 94).

24. Saariaho interview, March 16, 2002, Turku, Finland.

25. Saariaho cited in Robert Maycock, "Finnish Whispers," *Classical Music* (January 14, 1989).

26. Saariaho cited in Henry Bacon, "Musiikkia valon ja varjon rajamailta," *Rondo* 2 (1988): 10.

27. Wassily Kandinsky, *Concerning the Spiritual in the Art* (New York: Dover, 1977), as well as *Point and Line to Plane* (New York: Dover, 1979). Kandinsky had lively correspondence with the composer Arnold Schoenberg, who initiated correspondence in 1911, the year that *Concerning the Spiritual in the Art* was published. They both "hoped to abolish all that pertained to externality in the work of art, in order to open space to project a cosmic vibration." Cite from Daniel Albright, ed., *Modernism and Music: An Anthology with Sources* (Chicago: University of Chicago Press, 2004), 168.

28. Paul Klee, *Histoire naturelle infinie* (Schwarde & Co, 1977), and *Le pensée créatrice* (Schwarde & Co, 1980).

29. Interesting parallels between music and visual arts concerning other composers, such as Franz Schubert, Alexander Scriabin, Arnold Schoenberg, and Edgard Varèse, have been examined in *Music and Modern Art*, ed. James Leggio (London: Routledge , 2002).

30. An interesting comparison can be observed between the composer's multisensory perception and the five themes of the *La Dame à la Licorne* tapestry, which illustrate the five senses: sight, hearing, smell, taste, and touch. See Carl Nordenfalk, "Les Cinq sens dans l'art du Moyen Age," *Revue de l'art* 36 (1976): 17–28.

31. Kaija Saariaho, "Matter and Mind in Music",114.

32. Karttunen interview, March 14, 2002, Turku, Finland.

33. Ibid.

34. Saariaho, "Matter and Mind in Music," 114.

35. Saariaho interview, July 28, 1998, Helsinki, Finland.

36. Saariaho interview, December 6, 2000, Paris, France.

37. Ibid.

38. Saariaho cited in Bernard Mérigaud, "Sons et lumières," unknown source, from Saariaho's home archives.

39. The electronic and computational means used by Saariaho are, in the most illuminating and pedagogical way, demonstrated by Jean-Baptiste Barrière in the section "Spectrum" of *Prisma* CD-ROM (Helsinki: WSOY, 1999). This has also greatly supported my understanding of them.

40. Electro-acoustic music became a part of the Western art music canon after the Second World War, when atonality had challenged the dominant position of pitch. Computers—which do not produce sound—support the sound production and the digitalization of sound allows for more exactness by controlling complex combinations of musical parameters. For more, see *Modern Times. From World War I to the Present*, ed. Robert Morgan (Englewood Cliffs, N.J.: Prentice Hall, 1993).

41. Robert Morgan, *Twentieth-Century Music* (New York: Norton & Company, 1991), 479.

42. Robert Maycock, "Finnish Whispers." *Classical Music* (January 14,1989).

43. Andrew Clements, "Out of the Shadows," *Guardian* (August, 25,1995).

44. Paul Nelson, "The Uses of Electronics in Three Works by Kaija Saariaho" (May 10, 2004). http://pnelsoncomposer.com/writings/KaijaSaariahoAnalysis.html.

45. Saariaho cited in Danielle Cohen-Levinas, "Entretien avec Kaija Saariaho," *La synthèse sonore* 2, Les Cahiers de l'IRCAM 17 (Paris: IRCAM, 1993).

46. See Jean-Baptiste Barrière, *Prisma* CD-ROM (Helsinki: WSOY, 1999).

47. The programming was realized by Xavier Chabot and Jean-Baptiste Barrière at IRCAM.

48. Karttunen interview, March 16, 2001, Turku, Finland.

49. Karttunen, an email message to the author, October 18, 2006.

50. The term *soundscape* was introduced by a Canadian R. Murray Schafer to refer to the sounds of a place.

51. Taina Viljanen, *Jälkiä itsessä. Narratiivisia huilisti-identiteettejä Kaija Saariahon säveltämässä musiikissa* (Turku: Turun yliopisto, 2005).

52. Pitch-based score-followers cannot be used so far because of the many different playing techniques used in Saariaho's music.

CHAPTER 4: *Sounds*

1. Saariaho interview, November 21, 2001, Paris, France. All the interviews quoted in this chapter were made by the author, Pirkko Moisala.

2. Saariaho cited in Andrew Ford, "Just a Composer (Kaija Saariaho)," in *Composer to Composer*, ed. Andrew Ford (Sydney: Hale & Iremonger, 1993).

3. Saariaho cited in Kai Amberla, "Kaija Saariaho: Elämää musiikin kautta, musiikkia elämän kautta," *Rondo* 8 (1995): 4–7.

4. Robert Maycock, "Finnish Whispers," *Classical Music* 14 (1989).

5. Ibid.

6. Karttunen cited by Sara Norling in *Dagens Nyheter* (May 12, 2001).

7. Kent Nagano in STV, Swedish TV, in 2000.

8. Saariaho cited in *The Guardian* (August 25, 1995).

9. Saariaho cited in Pierre Michel, "Entretien avec Kaija Saariaho. Kaija Saariaho," *Compositeurs d'aujourd'hui* 6, ed. Risto Nieminen. Les cahiers de l'Ircam (Paris: IRCAM, Centre Georges-Pompidou, 1994), 9.

10. Karttunen interview, November 27, 2001, Paris, France.

11. See Joel Chabade, *Electric Sound: The Past and Promise of Electronic Music* (Englewood Cliffs, N.J.: Prentice Hall, 1997).

12. Karttunen cited in Cori Ellison, "Uncovering Beauty in Ordinary Noise," *New York Times* (November 7, 1999).

13. Luigi Russola, "The Art of Noises: Futurist Manifesto (1913)," in *Modernism and Music*, ed. Paul Albright (Chicago: University of Chicago Press. 2004), 177–83. Tanja Uimola has also examined the futurist features of Saariaho's aesthetics in her article "Futuristisia piirteitä Kaija Saariahon estetiikassa," in *Elektronisia unelmia*, ed. Anne Sivuoja-Gunaratnam (Helsinki: Yliopistopaino, 2005), 23–48.

14. Russola, "The Art of Noises: Futurist Manifesto (1913)"

15. Ibid.

16. Karttunen interview, November 27, 2001, Paris, France.

17. Florent Jodelet, "Entretien, Kaija Saariaho The Queen of Finland . . . in Japan," in unknown newspaper from Saariaho's home archives, 21–24.

18. Tomi Mäkelä, "Talks about Texture, Viewpoints on Orchestration," *Finnish Music Quarterly* 2 (1992): 43.

19. Karttunen interview, March 14, 2002, Turku, Finland.

20. Saariaho in *The Times* (October 30, 2001).

21. Tristan Murail, "Spectra and Pixies," *Contemporary Music Review* 1 (1984): 157–70.

22. Vesa Kankaanpää's thesis of the licenciat examines the organization of sound color in Saariaho's work of the 1980s. Vesa Kankaanpää, *Sointivärin organisaatio Kaija Saariahon sävellyksissä* (unpublished thesis, Turku University, 1996).

23. Saariaho interview, November 21, 2001, Paris, France.

24. Ibid.

25. Stephen MacAdams and Kaija Saariaho, "Qualities and Functions of Musical Timbre," in *Proceedings of the International Computer Music Conference* (San Francisco: Computer Music Association, 1985), 367–74.

26. Salonen phone interview, September 15, 2006

27. Saariaho cited by Craig Smith, *The New Mexican,* date unknown, from Saariaho's home archives.

28. Saariaho cited in Liisa Hautsalo, "Sliding in Sound—Material and Immaterial Images in Kaija Saariaho's Flute Music," *Finnish Music Quarterly* 1 (2003): 32.

29. Karttunen interview, November 27, 2001, Paris, France. According to him, the cellists speak of "deformed sound," while—for the listener—it sounds like a broken sound.

30. Karttunen interview, January 27, 2001, Paris, France.

31. Ibid.

32. Saariaho interview, December 6, 2001, Paris, France.

33. Taina Riikonen, *Jälkiä itsessä. Narratiivisia huilisti-identiteettejä Kaija Saariahon säveltämässä musiikissa* (Turku: Turun yliopisto, 2005), 35. Riikonen interviewed three flutists about flutist identities constructed by Saariaho's music.

34. Bruno Bartolozzi, *New Sounds for Woodwind,* 2nd ed. (Oxford: Oxford University Press. 1982/1967); and J. Chabade, *Electric Sound. The Past and Promise of Electronic Music* (Englewood Cliffs, N.J.: Prentice Hall, 1997), 23.

35. Riikonen, *Jälkiä itsessä. Narratiivisia huilisti-identiteettejä Kaija Saariahon säveltämässä musiikissa* (2005), 132.

36. Eirola interview, April 4, 2002, Turku, Finland.

37. From "Oiseaux (Birds), XIII," trans. Robert Fitzgerald, in *Poems by Saint-John Perse,* Complete Collection (Princeton: Princeton University Press 1983), 609–39. "Neiges (Snow)" and "Amers (Seamarks)" from the same collection of poems relate to Saariaho's works of the same names as well.

38. Saariaho cited in Joëlle Gardes Tamine, "Dans l'inspiration des images", *Revue des deux mondes* (March 1999): 118–19.

39. More on *NoaNoa,* in Taina Riikonen, "Shaken or Stirred—Virtual Reverberation

Spaces and Transformative Gender Identities in Kaija Saariaho's *NoaNoa* (1992) for Flute and Electronics," *Organised Sound* 8(1) (2003):109–15.

40. Hoitenga interview, January 27, 2002, Turku, Finland.

41. Ibid.

42. Translated by Kitty Hunter-Blair, ODE 804–2.

43. Eirola interview, April 4, 2002, Turku, Finland.

44. Saariaho in a lecture at the Sibelius Academy, April 30, 1998, Helsinki, Finland.

45. Liisamaija Hautsalo, "Simply Unadorned and Crystal-Clear [L'amour de loin]," *Finnish Music Quarterly* 3–4, (2000).

46. Saariaho interview, October 21, 2005, Vilnius, Lithuania.

47. Since Mattila gained international fame by winning the Cardiff Singer of the World Competition in 1983, she has performed at the most distinguished opera houses as well as in major concert houses.

48. Karita Mattila in *Helsingin Sanomat* (August 25, 2006).

49. Saariaho interview, December 6, 2000, Paris, France.

50. Kaija Saariaho, "Timbre and Harmony: Interpolations of Timbral Structures," *Contemporary Music Review* 2(1) (1987): 93.

51. Comp. with Michel, Pierre: "Entretien avec Kaija Saariaho," *Kaija Saariaho. Compositeurs d'aujourd'hui* 6, ed. Risto Nieminen (Paris: Ircam—Centre Georges-Pompidou, 1994), 16.

52. Gérald Grisey, "La Musique: le Devenir de Sons," *La Revue Musicale* (1991): 291–300.

53. Saariaho, "Timbre and Harmony," 97.

54. Ivanka Stoianova, "Spectra," *Prisma* CD-ROM, *The Musical World of Kaija Saariaho* (Helsinki: WSOY, 1999).

55. Ibid.

56. Kai Amberla, "Kaija Saariaho: Elämää musiikin kautta, musiikkia elämän kautta," *Rondo* 8 (1995): 6.

57. Saariaho cited in Marja Dahlström, *Muodosta minuuteen* (Helsinki: Edita, 1999), 87–88.

58. Saariaho in the program notes for *Nymphea.*

59. Kimmo Korhonen, *Finnish Orchestral Music and Concertos 1995–2005* (Vaajakoski: Finnish Music Information Center. 2006), 83.

60. Saariaho: "Matter and Mind in Music." - *Matter and Mind in Architecture.* ed. Pirkko Tuukkanen (Hämeenlinna: Karisto, 2000), 111.

CHAPTER 5: *Dramas*

1. Unless otherwise stated, all the quotations from Peter Sellars are from the same interview, November 24, 2006, Vienna, Austria. All the quoted interviews in this chapter were made by the author, Pirkko Moisala.

2. Sellars in the program "*L'amour de loin*—Kaija Saariaho," on Swedish TV, 2003.

3. Saariaho in Anders Beyer, "Till Death Us Do Part. A Portrait of the Finnish Composer Kaija Saariaho," *Nordic Sounds* 1 (2000): 8.

4. Liisamaija Hautsalo, *Kerroksellisuus ja transelementit Kaija Saariahon Kaukainen rakkaus-oopperassa* (unpublished Phil.Lic. thesis, University of Helsinki 2006), 40–43. The thesis has been developed into a book *Kaukainen rakkaus. Saavuttamattomuuden semantiikka Kaija Saariahon oopperassa.* (Helsinki. Yliopistopaino, 2008).

5. Hautsalo, *Kerroksellisuus ja transelementit Kaija Saariahon Kaukainen rakkaus-oopperassa,* 75–87.

6. Saariaho, letter to the author, May 25, 2007.

7. Hautsalo, *Kerroksellisuus ja transelementit Kaija Saariahon Kaukainen rakkaus-oopperassa,* 40–43.

8. Liisamaija Hautsalo, "Kaipausta yliaistilliseen," program book to accompany the production of *L'amour de loin* at the Finnish National Opera (Helsinki: Kansallisooppera, 2004), 18–19.

9. Sellars on Swedish TV, February 2004. "Kaija Saariaho—*L'amour de loin.*"

10. These observations made about the role of the orchestra owe thanks to the interview with conductor Susanna Mälkki, October 26, 2004, Helsinki, Finland.

11. Saariaho, October 25, 2005, Vilnius, Lithuania.

12. Sanna Iitti, "Lámour de loin: Kaija Saariaho's First Opera," *Journal of the IAWM (International Alliance for Women in Music)* 8(1–2) (2002): 9–14.

13. Saariaho has removed the second piano from the revised version of the opera.

14. Saariaho in *The Full Score* (Winter 2005).

15. Saariaho in *Opera* (March 2006): 287.

16. Ibid.

17. Saariaho in Liisamaija Hautsalo, "The Sufferings of Young Adriana," *Finnish Music Quarterly* 1 (2006): 38.

18. Maalouf in *Washington Post,* March 28, 2006.

19. Saariaho, letter to the author, May 29, 2007.

20. Gustave Thibon, "Postschrift, Fifty Years Later," *Gravity and Grace* by Simone Weil, trans. Emma Crawford and Mario von der Ruhr (London and New York: Routledge, 1947/2002), 183.

21. Weil, *Gravity and Grace,* 130.

22. Sellars, November 26, 2006, Künstler Hause, Vienna, Austria.

23. Weil, *Gravity and Grace,* 4.

24. Sellars interview, November 24, 2006, Vienna, Austria.

25. Saariaho in a lecture, January 13, 1999, Stuttgart, Germany.

26. *Sisu* (guts) has a special position in the Finnish mythology, according to which the Finns are proud of having lots of *sisu.* A Finnish proverb states: "Guts is what takes one through a grey stone."

27. From an unpublished interview held in Saariaho's home archives.

28. Saariaho in *The Guardian* (August 25, 1995).

29. Weil, *Gravity and Grace,* 131.

30. Kaija Saariaho, "Musiikissa, musiikista, musiikkiin," in *Ammatti: säveltäjä 2006,* ed. Pekka Hako and Risto Nieminen (Helsinki: Like, 2006), 129.

31. Saariaho in *Finnish Music Quarterly* (March 14, 2007).

32. Saariaho in a lecture given in the University of California, San Diego, 1999.

33. Weil, *Gravity and Grace,* 149.

SELECTED WORKS

ONLY THE NAMES of the operas have official English translations.

Lichtbogen (Arches of Light; 1985–86) for flute, percussion, harp, piano, two violins, viola, cello, double bass, and live electronics.
Nymphea (Waterlily; 1987) for string quartet and live electronics.
Stilleben (Still Life; 1987–88), radiophonic work for tape, to the collage of texts by Franz Kafka, Paul Eluard, and Wassily Kandinsky.
Du cristal . . . à la Fumée (From Crystal . . . to the Smoke; 1989–90) for orchestra
Château de l'âme (The Castle of Soul; 1995) for solo soprano, eight female voices, and orchestra, to Indian and Egyptian poetry.
Lonh (Afar; 1996) for soprano and electronics to the text by Jaufré Rudel.
L'amour de loin (Love from Afar; 1999–2000), opera; libretto by Amin Maalouf.
Aile du Songe (The Wing of Dream; 2000–2001) for flute and orchestra.
Quatre instants (Four Moments; 2002) for soprano and piano (also written also for orchestra), to the text by Amin Maalouf.
Adriana Mater (2004–5), opera; libretto by Amin Maalouf.
La Passion de la Simone (Simone's Passions 2005), oratorio; libretto by Amin Maalouf.
Notes on Light (2007), cello concerto.

SELECTED LISTENING

EXTRACTS OF SAARIAHO'S WORKS can be found on the Internet. For instance, the web page of her publisher (www.chesternovello.com) provides several examples. Visual concerts, a multimedia show, and an installation based on Saariaho's works, created by Jean-Babtiste Barrière, can be found at the composer's home pages (www.saariaho.org). Web pages of the record company Petals (www.petals.org), run among others by Saariaho, as well as YouTube are also worth checking.

Adjö, Ondine ODE 958–2 (2000).
Aile du songe, Montaigne MO 782154 (2002).
Amers, Sony Music SK 60817 (2001).
Die Aussicht, Ondine ODE 958–2 (2000).
Caliban's Dream, Ondine ODE 958–2 (2000).
Cendres, Mode Records mode 91 (2000), Kairos 0012412KAI (2004)
Château de l'âme, Sony Music SK 60817 (2001).
Cinq reflets, Ondine ODE 1049–2 (2004).
Cloud Music, Petals Petal003 (1998).
Du gick, flög, Ondine ODE 958–2 (2000).
Du Cristal . . . à la Fumée, Ondine ASIN: B0002D9E48 (2004).
From the Grammar of Dreams, Ondine ODE 958–2 (2000).
Graal théâtre, Sony Music SK 60817 (2001).
Grammaire des rêves, Mode Records mode 91 (2000), Ondine ODE 958–2 (2000).
Il pleut, Ondine ODE 958–2 (2000).
Io, Finlandia 1576533742 (FACD 374) (1989), Finlandia Records 3984–23407–2 (1999).
Jardin secret I, BIS-CD-307 (1997).
Jardin secret II, Finlandia Records 3984–23407–2 (1999).
Laconisme de l'aile, BIS-CD-307 (1997), Montaigne MO 782154 (2002), Kairos 0012412KAI (2004).
L'amour de loin at the Finnish National Opera, DVD 004400734026 (NTSC format; 2004).
Lichtbogen, Finlandia 1576533742 (FACD 374) (1989), Finlandia 3984–23407–2 (1999).
La Dame à la Licorne, Petals Petal 003 (1998).

Lonh, Ondine ODE 906–2 (1997).
Mirage, Ondine ODE 1130–2 (2008).
Miranda's Lament, Ondine ODE 958–2 (2000).
Mirrors, Kairos 0012412KAI (2004), Aeon AECD 0637 (2006).
Monkey fingers, Kairos 0012412KAI (2004).
Neiges, Petals Petal 005 (2000).
New Gates, Mode Records mode 91 (2000).
NoaNoa, BIS-CD-307 (1997), Ondine ODE 906–2 (1997), Ondine ODE 906–2 (1997), Kairos 0012412KAI (2004).
Notes on Light, Ondine ODE 1130–2 (2008).
Nymphea Reflection, Ondine ODE 1049–2 (2004).
Oi Kuu, Aeon AECD 0637 (2006).
Oltra Mar, Ondine ODE 1049–2 (2004).
Orion, Ondine ODE 1130–2 (2008).
Petals, Petals Petal 001 (1997), Finlandia Records 3984–23407–2 (1999), Aeon AECD 0637 (2006).
Près, Petals Petal 001 (1997), Aeon AECD 0637 (2006).
Spins and Spells, Petals Petal 001 (1997), Aeon AECD 0637 (2006).
Sept Papillions, Aeon AECD 0637 (2006).
Poèmes de Saint-John Perse, Montaigne MO 782154 (2002).
Preludi-Tunnustus-Postludi, Ondine ODE 958–2 (2000).
Près, Ondine ODE 906–2 (1997).
. . . sah den Vögeln, BIS-CD-307 (1997).
Sept Papillons, Ondine ASIN: B0002D9E48 (2004).
Six Japanese Gardens, Ondine ODE 906–2 (1997), Kairos 0012412KAI (2004).
Solar, Mode Records mode 91 (2000).
Spins and Spells, Kairos 0012412KAI (2004).
Stilleben. Finlandia 1576533742 (FACD 374) (1989), Finlandia 3984–23407–2 (1999).
Velvet Hand, Kairos 0012412KAI (2004).
Verblendungen, Finlandia 1576533742 (FACD 374) (1989), BIS-CD-307 (1997), Finlandia Records 3984–23407–2 (1999).

FOR FURTHER READING

Beck, Stephen David. 1992. "Lichtbogen, Io, Verblendungen, Stilleben FACD 374, Finlandia Records." *Computer Music Journal* 16(4): 92–93.

Fineberg, Joshua (ed.). 2000. "Spectral Music: Aesthetics and Music." *Contemporary Music Review* 19(3).

Finnish Music Information Center (FIMIC). www.fimic.fi.

Finnish Music Quarterly (see www.fimic.fi). Various issues include several articles on Saariaho.

Hautsalo, Liisamaija. 2000. "Simply Unadorned and Crystal-Clear [L'Amour de loin]." *Finnish Music Quarterly* 2000(3–4).

Iitti, Sanna. 2001. "Stylistic Development and Artistic Principles." *Journal of the IAWM (International Alliance for Women in Music)* 7(3): 17–20.

Kankaanpää, Vesa, 1996. "Displaced Time: Transcontextual References to Time in Kaija Saariaho's Stilleben." *Organised Sound* 1(2): 87–92.

Mäkelä, Tomi. "Saariaho." *Musik in Geschichte und Gegenwart, Personenteil 14* (Ric-Schön). Zweite, neuarbeitete Ausgabe, hrsg. v. Ludvig Finscher. Stuttgart: Bärenreiter, 2005. Pp. 732–38.

Moisala, Pirkko. 2000. "Gender Negotiation of the Composer Kaija Saariaho in Finland: The Woman Composer as Nomadic Subject." In *Music and Gender*, edited by Pirkko Moisala and Beverly Diamond. Urbana and Chicago: University of Illinois Press. Pp. 166–88.

Prisma CD-ROM (1998; ISBN 951–0–24532–1; Helsinki: WSOY).

Riikonen, Taina. 2003. "Shaken or Stirred—Virtual Reverberation Spaces and Transformative Gender Identities in Kaija Saariaho's NoaNoa (1992) for Flute and Electronics." *Organized Sound. An International Journal of Music Technology* 8(1):109–17.

Saariaho, Kaija. 1987. "Timbre and Harmony: Interpolations of Timbral Structures." *Contemporary Music Review* 1(2): 93–133.

Sivuoja-Gunaratnam, Anne. 1998. "Rhetoric of Transition in Kaija Saariaho's Music." In *Musical Signification: Between Rhetoric and Pragmatics. Proceedings of the 5th International Congress on Musical Signification*, edited by Gino Stefani, Eero Tarasti, and Luca Marconi. Bologna: CLUEB, 1998. Pp. 537–542.

———. 2003. "Desire and distance in Kaija Saariaho's Lonh." *Organized Sound. An International Journal of Music Technology* 8(1): 71–85.

INDEX

Aaltoila, Heikki, 16, 110n35, 110n39
acoustics, 8, 11, 63, 69, 71
Albright, Daniel, 115n27, 116n13
Amberla, Kai, 20, 111n48, 114n13, 116n3, 118n56
amplification, 33, 37, 43, 48, 67, 68, 70, 71, 85, 86, 100, 106
Ars Electronica Festival, 16
Ashley, Tim, 48, 113n58
Atlan, Henri, 112n27
avant-garde, 7, 77

Bach, Johann Sebastian, 1, 76
Bacon, Henry, 115n26
Bakhtin, Mikhail, vii
Barbican Center, 18, 24
Barrière, Jean-Baptiste, vii, 14, 15, 19, 115n39, 116nn46–47
Bartolozzi, Bruno, 117n34
Beethoven, Ludwig von, 4
Beigler, Doris and Myron, 16
Berg, Alban, 77
Bergman, Erik, 76
Berio, Luciano, 76
Berlioz, Hector, 6, 36
Beyer, Anders, 110n45, 111n52, 118n3
Bibliothèque Nationale (Paris), 43
Björling, Gunnar, 86
body, bodily, 1, 15, 35, 52, 56, 57, 58, 63, 84–85, 87, 91–92
Born, Georgina, 110n31
Boulez, Pierre, 9, 14
bowing, 13, 33, 68, 78, 80–81. *See also* playing techniques
Brahms, Johannes, 80
Braque, Georges, 83
Burton, Humbrey, 46, 113n49
Bye, Anthony, 34, 112n17

Canetti, Elias, 30
CARL (California Academic and Research Libraries), 18
Carlin, Francis, 50, 113n64
Carlson, Carolyn, 60
Center for Computer Music and Music Technology, Tokyo, 18
Chabade, Joel, 116n11, 117n34
Chabot, Xavier, 110n32, 116n47
Citron, Marcia, 109n8
Clements, Andrew, 39, 67, 112n31, 116n43
Cohen-Levinas, Danielle, 116n45
collaborations, 21, 54, 65, 78, 80, 84–85, 87, 93. *See also* Hoitenga, Camilla; Karttunen, Anssi
color. *See under* sound
composition techniques, 5, 11, 12, 14, 30, 32, 33, 34, 41, 44, 53, 54, 61, 67, 73
Cytowic, Richard E., 114n10

Dahlström, Marja, 114n14, 118n57
La Dame à la Licorne tapestry, 115n30
Darmstadt, 8, 15, 21
Davidson, Justin, 48, 113n56
Debussy, Claude, 8, 10, 47, 76, 100

Department of musicology, Helsinki University, 8
Donatoni, Franco, 8
Dyer, Richard, 42, 112n35

Ears Open! (Korvat auki!), 7, 21
echo, 2, 3, 43, 67, 68
Eirola (née Raitio), Anne, vii, 83, 117n36, 118n45
electronics, electronic, 12, 25, 31, 40, 44, 46, 65–72, 92, 99, 100, 101, 106; filters, 39, 34, 43, 68, 70; live (*see* live electronics); music, 8; part, 39, 40, 71, 104; optional, 30, 57, 82; tools, means, 8, 26, 30, 32, 34, 46, 65. *See also* amplification; harmonizer; live electronics; reverberation; sound; spatialization
Eliot, T. S., 29
Ellison, Cori, 47, 110n22, 111n56, 113n53, 116n12
Eluard, Paul, 86
expressionism, 73

feminine, femininity, 6, 8, 16, 28
Ferneyhough, Brian, 8, 83
Fleming, Shirley, 46, 47, 113n52, 113n46
film, 19, 29, 59, 74, 85
FIMIC (Finnish Music Information Center), 16
Finch, Hilary, 46, 113n50
Finland, Finnish culture, 5, 7, 8, 9, 10, 16, 17, 19, 20, 29, 35–36, 37, 41, 42, 48, 54, 74, 109n7, 119n26
Finnish Broadcasting Corporation, 16, 17, 32
Ford, Andrew, 37, 111n4, 112n29, 116n12
form, musical, 7, 9, 16, 27, 30, 31, 34, 36, 38, 40, 56–58, 62, 65, 74, 77, 88–92, 104, 107
France, French culture, 9–10, 13–15, 20, 29, 34, 42–43, 74, 77, 103
Freeman, Robin, 15, 110n36
Freiburg Musikhochschule, 8
French National Opera. *See* Opéra Bastille
futurism, 73, 76, 77, 88

Gauguin, Paul, 56
gender and sex, 8, 14, 16, 17, 27
Genet-Bondeville, Caroline, 114–115n23
Germany, German culture, 9, 10, 11, 23, 34
Gervasoni, Pierre, 48, 113n59
gesture, musical, 27, 33, 61, 68, 75, 92, 98, 99, 106
Goethe, Johann Wolfgang von, 58
Gonzáles-Arroyon, Ramón, 110n32
Grabócz, Márta, 112n14
Grisey, Gerard, 8, 10, 11, 76, 110n25, 118n52
GRM (Groupe de Recherches Musicales), 12, 13

Haas, Georg Friedrich, 11
Hamilton, Andy, 111n8
harmonizer, 33, 67, 70
harmony, harmonic, 10, 11, 12, 13, 21, 27, 30, 31, 32, 34, 36–39, 61, 66, 68, 78, 88
Hautsalo, Liisamaija, 97, 113n61, 117n28, 118n45, 119nn4–5, 119nn7–8, 119n17
Hedblad, Lars, 111n9
Heikinheimo, Seppo, 8, 15, 109n16, 109n17, 110n34
Heininen, Paavo, 5, 6
Helsinki Rudolf Steiner School, 2, 4
Henken, John, 112n24
Hettmansberger, Greg, 37, 112n28
Hoitenga, Camilla, vii, 9, 20, 65, 84, 92, 110n20, 118n40
Hölderlin, Friedrich, 87
Huber, Klaus, 8
Huddersfield Contemporary Music Festival, 16, 46

identity, 14, 19, 73, 104
Iitti, Sanna, 100, 119n12
impressionism, 45, 73, 75, 76–77, 86, 99, 100
Indian music, 74
Institute for Music/Acoustic Research and Coordination. *See* IRCAM
Institute of Industrial Arts and Crafts, Helsinki, 4

instrumental writing, 35, 36
instrumentation, 29, 45, 61, 78
interpolation, 12, 30, 32, 33, 67
IRCAM (Institute for Music/Acoustic Research and Coordination), 9, 11, 12, 13, 14, 16, 19, 21, 25, 43, 69
Isopuro, Jukka, 28, 111n3
L'Itinéraire, 10, 11

Japan, Japanese culture, 17, 18–19, 74, 84
Jodelet, Florent, 110n43, 117n17

Kafka, Franz, 35
Kandinsky, Wassily, 32, 54, 58–59, 88, 90, 115n27
Kankaanpää, Vesa, 117n22
Karelia, 1, 86
Karttunen, Anssi, vii; cited, 110n30, 114n7, 114n19, 115n32, 116nn48–49, 116n6, 116n10, 116n12, 117n16, 117n19, 117nn29–30; collaboration with Saariaho, 13, 20, 33, 65, 80–81; on Saariaho's music, 55, 60, 68, 71, 75–77, 82
Kekkonen, Urho, 17
Kennedy Center, 48
Klee, Paul, 58, 115n28
Kokkonen, Joonas, 7, 17
Korhonen, Kimmo, 90, 114n18, 118n59
Korvat auki! (Ears Open!), 7, 21
Kozinn, Allan, 112n37
Kremer, Gidon, 39
Kronos Quartet, 16
Kunitachi College of Music, 19
Kurz, Michael, 111n1, 113n1

Laakkonen, Launo, 1, 4
Laakkonen, Tuovi, 1, 4
Leggio, James, 115n29
Leiviskä, Helvi, 5
Ligeti, György, 55, 76–77
Liimatainen, Jussi, vii, 7, 32, 112n13
Lincoln Center, 16, 18, 24
Lindberg, Magnus, 6, 21
live electronics, 32, 33, 34, 37, 38, 43, 46, 54, 65, 70, 71, 92
Lutoslawski, Witold, 48
Lyytikäinen, Olli, 5

Maalouf, Amin, 22, 23, 24, 45, 95, 101, 102, 103–4, 119n18
Macassar, Gilles, 22, 111n60
Maillard, Benedict, 69
Mäkelä, Tomi, 117n18
Malka, Raija, 20
Mälkki, Susanna, vii, 119n10
Mattila, Karita, 48, 87, 118nn47–48
Maycock, Robert, 75, 115n25, 116n42, 116n4
McAdams, Steven, 14, 79, 117n25
melody, 12, 27, 36, 37, 38, 39, 40, 44, 47, 48, 50, 51, 61, 67, 86, 91, 92, 98, 99, 106
Mérigaud, Bernard, 115n38
Messiaen, Olivier, 10, 21, 22, 45, 46, 54, 76–77, 100
Michel, Pierre, 110n19, 116n9, 118n51
microtonality, 11, 66, 98
Millington, Barry, 36, 112n25
minimalism, 11
Moberg, Ida, 4
Monet, Claude, 58, 60, 114n23
Morgan, Robert, 110n28, 115nn40–41
Mortier, Gerard, 21, 23
Mozart, Wolfgang Amadeus, 4, 22
Mozart Festwochen, Vienna, 50
Murail, Tristan, 8, 10, 11, 76, 110n24, 117n21
Murray, David, 45, 113n43
Murto, Ana, vii
Musée national du Moyen Age—Thermes de Cluny, 60
musical gesture. *See* gesture, musical
musical language, 6, 11, 22, 30, 52, 65, 106
musicians, performing Saariaho's music, 70, 71, 75, 79–80, 81, 82, 85, 87. *See also* collaborations
musicology, 4, 5
musique concrète, 12, 13, 70

Nagano, Kent, 75, 116n7

nature, 9, 11, 13, 18, 32, 56, 57, 58, 59, 76. *See also under* sound
Nellens, Kathy, vii, 111n59
Nelson, Paul, 67, 116n44
Nieminen, Risto, 16, 110n19, 110n38, 114n9, 114n11, 116n9, 118n51
Nin, Anaïs, 5
noise, 14, 30, 32, 33, 51, 56, 66, 67, 75, 76, 79, 81, 85, 100
Nordenfalk, Carl, 115n30
Nordic, Northernness, 29, 48
Norling, Sara, 166n6
Nuorvala, Juhani, 11n2

Oestreich, James R., 47, 113n54
Olgan, Olivier, 50, 113n65
opera, 22–24, 25, 27, 40, 42, 45, 46, 49, 50, 93–103
Opéra Bastille (French National Opera), 23–24, 29, 49, 50
orchestra, orchestral, 21, 27, 30, 35, 36, 37, 40, 45, 46, 49
orchestration, 32, 39, 40, 46, 50, 57, 74, 86, 92, 93, 94, 99, 100, 102, 106
overtone, 10, 39, 66, 68, 80

Page, Tim, 48, 113n60
perception (of music), 10, 11, 14, 31, 34, 43, 56, 60, 74, 78, 79, 80
Perse, Saint-John, 30, 39, 83–84, 92, 114n17, 117n37
Persichetti, Vincent, 5
Pettitt, Stephen, 38, 112n30
Plath, Sylvia, 5, 86
playing techniques, 11, 34, 37, 39, 48, 61, 63, 78, 85, 106. *See also* bowing
polyphony, 39, 40, 67, 85, 88
polyrhythm, 19
Pompidou, Georges, 9
post-serialism, 5, 7, 8, 10
Potard, Yves, 12
Pribil, H. D., 45, 113n45
processed sound. *See* sound: processing, processed
Proust, Marcel, 10
pulse. *See* rhythm, pulse

Radio France, 12
Raitio, Anne. *See* Eirola (née Raitio), Anne
Ravel, Maurice, 8, 10, 76–77
Ravinia Festival, 47
recorded sound. *See* sound: recorded
Reinvere, Juri, 110n21
reverberation, 33, 38, 67, 68, 70, 86, 101
Rhein, John von, 49, 113n62
rhythm, pulse, 27, 29, 32, 33, 35, 38, 39, 40, 44, 47, 49, 50, 56, 57, 61, 60, 78, 89, 90, 91–92
Rich, Alan, 33, 112n15
Riding, Alan, 50, 113n63
Riikonen (née Viljanen), Taina, 69–70, 116n51, 117n33, 117n35, 117n39
Roddy, Michael, 111n65
Rodet, Xavier, 12
role models, 5–6
romantic music, 74, 77, 100
Ross, Alex, 47, 50, 113n67, 113n68
Roubaud, Jacques, 39, 43, 86, 112n33, 112n37
Rudel, Jaufré, 43
Russolo, Luigi, 76, 116n13, 117n14

Saariaho, Kaija: awards, 15, 17–18, 20, 23; characteristics of music, 73–93; childhood, 1–4, 9–10; commissions, 16, 17–18, 23–25; process of composing, 44, 52–65, 105; reception, 8, 15–17, 22, 28, 31, 33–39, 42–51; use of technology, 54–55, 65–72
—compositional periods: early years, 7–16, 26, 29–30; musical gestures, 27, 38–45; prime years, 17–25, 27–29, 45–51, 104–7; sound laboratory, 14, 26, 30–32; timbre, 27, 32–37; transitional period, 27, 38
—works by: *Adjö,* 86; *Adriana Mater,* 24, 25, 27, 48, 49–50, 54, 70, 92, 95, 101–3, 104, 106; *Aile du songe,* 48, 49, 54, 83, 84, 91–92; *Amers,* 18, 38–39, 56–57, 70, 89, 90; *L'amour de loin,* vii, 21, 22, 23, 27, 45–47, 49, 50, 64, 70, 75, 92, 94, 96–100, 102, 104; *Die Aussicht,* 87; *Bruden,* 29; *Caliban's Dream,* 86, 87; *Cartolina per*

Siena, 8; *Château de l'âme*, 18, 21, 28, 40–43, 54, 87, 91; *Cinq reflets de L'amour de loin*, 48; *La Dame à la Licorne*, 60, 65, 69; *Dolce tormento*, 48; *Du Cristal*, 17, 18, 27, 35–37, 39, 54, 82, 91, 92, 102; *Du gick, flög*, 86; . . . *à la Fumée*, 17, 36–37, 38, 39, 64, 82, 85, 92; *From the Grammar of Dreams*, 16, 60, 86, 94; *Graal théâtre*, 18, 29, 39–40, 54, 64, 65, 90; *Grammaire des rêves*, 86; *Im Träume*, 88, 91; *Io*, 16; *Jardin secret I*, 30, 90; *Jardin secret II*, 12, 32, 65, 85, 90; *Laconisme de l'aile*, 9, 30, 57, 80, 84, 92; *Lichtbogen*, 16, 32–33, 34, 60, 61, 85, 89, 90; *Lonh*, 18, 21, 23, 40, 43–45, 54, 71, 87, 90, 91; *Maa*, 13, 27, 37–38, 57, 60, 70, 94; *Miranda's Lament*, 86; *Neiges*, 75, 91; *NoaNoa*, 54, 69, 83, 84; *Nocturne*, 48; *Notes on Light*, 54, 92, 106; *Nuits, adieux*, 18, 70, 86, 87; *Nymphea*, 16, 29, 33–34, 56, 58, 60, 85, 90, 92; *Nymphea Reflection*, 92; *Oltra Mar*, 18, 45, 65, 92; *Orion*, 49, 65, 90, 92; *La Passion de Simone*, 24, 25, 49–50, 103–4; *Petals*, 34, 54, 68, 69, 81–82, 91; *Preludi-Tunnustus-Postludi*, 86; *Près*, 54, 56, 58, 70; *Prospero's Vision*, 87; *Quatre instants*, 48, 87; . . . *sah den Vögeln*, 30, 78, 83, 86; *Sept Papillions*, 47–48, 54, 91; *Six Japanese Gardens*, 18–19, 74, 90; *Solar*, 38, 90; *Spins and Spells*, 54, 82; *Stilleben*, 13, 16, 34–35, 54, 70; *Suomenkielinen sekakuorokappale*, 29; *Verblendungen*, 12, 14, 15, 30, 31, 32, 61, 65, 88
Saariaho, Markku, 5
Said, Abou, 45
Sallinen, Aulis, 7
Salonen, Esa-Pekka, vii, 7, 21, 36, 79, 94, 109n11, 112n24, 117n26
Salzburg Music Festival, 18, 21, 22, 42, 45
San Diego, 27, 35, 107
Sandner, Wolfgang, 46, 113n44
Santa Fe Music Festival, 22, 46, 48
Saraste, Jukka-Pekka, 6
Schaefer, R. Murray, 116n50
Schaeffer, Pierre, 13
Schluren, Christopher, 42, 112n36
Schoenberg, Arnold, 77, 115n27, 115n29
Schopenhauer, Arthur, 56, 114n16
Schubert, Franz, 115n29
Schumann, Clara, 4
score, vii, 9, 60, 63, 64, 71–72, 75, 81, 84–85
Scriabin, Alexander, 115n29
Seckerson, Edward, 35, 112n22
self-image, 4, 6, 9–10, 19, 20, 28, 97
Sellars, Peter, vii, 22, 23, 24, 40, 93–94, 96, 99, 103, 104, 111n59, 118n1, 118n3, 119n9, 119n22, 119n24
senses, 6, 16, 52–53, 55–56, 60, 93, 105, 115n30
serialism, 11, 73, 77, 96
Shakespeare, William, 86
Sibelius, Jean, 4, 5, 29, 36, 37, 38, 41, 54, 76, 80, 111n47
Sibelius Academy, Helsinki, 6, 8, 19, 26, 28
Silverton, Mike, 32, 111n12
Sirén, Vesa, 100n23
Sivuoja-Gunaratnam, Anne, vii, 35, 112n20, 112n34, 116n13
Smith, Craig, 113n51, 117n27
Södergran, Edith, 5, 29
song text, 5, 22, 23, 24, 25, 29, 30, 35, 39, 41–42, 43, 44, 45, 50, 59, 86, 104
sonority, 10, 11, 32, 44, 48, 99
sound, 10, 11, 19, 21, 33, 57, 72, 77–87; analysis and study of, 10–11, 12, 13, 14, 26, 30, 32, 41, 54, 65, 66–67, 74, 79; categorization of, 13, 57–58, 78–79; color, 4, 10, 17, 27, 29, 32, 36, 37, 40, 45, 47, 48, 52, 57, 61, 74, 77–88, 92, 94, 106; electronic (*see* electronics, electronic); field, 30, 76, 79, 99–102; living, 12, 13, 59, 63, 74; masses of, 33, 36, 45, 90; natural, 13, 34, 38, 57, 63, 65, 70; of nature, 2, 9, 13, 38, 43, 44, 48, 69, 86; processing, processed, 13, 26, 34, 39, 40, 43, 54, 65, 67, 68, 101, 102; recorded, 13, 33, 34, 40, 44, 54, 58, 66; and space; 67–70; spectra, 10, 33, 66; stereo, 35; synthesis, synthetic, 12, 13, 30, 54, 65, 66, 67, 68, 69; technician, 14, 62, 71, 80

soundscapes, 38, 43, 65, 69–70, 87, 98–99, 116n50
Spano, Robert, 46, 113n51
spatiality, 43, 78, 88, 90, 99, 106
spatialization, 43, 69, 70, 92, 93
spectral harmony, 10, 11, 61
spectralism, 10, 11, 13, 36, 38, 61, 73–74, 77, 99, 100, 109n18
spirituality, 24, 40, 47, 58, 59, 60, 75, 93, 98, 100, 103–4, 105
Steiner, Rudolf, 2–3, 4, 109n7, 114n14
Stockhausen, Karl-Heinz, 9, 78
Stoianova, Ivanka, 39, 88, 112n32, 118n54
Story, John, 44, 113n41
Stravinsky, Igor, 29, 76
Strozzi, Barbara, 4
structure, 9, 13, 31, 34, 36, 37, 39, 43, 44, 59, 62, 74, 75
studio work, 8, 14, 25, 32, 34, 62, 72
Summer Sounds Festival, 7
synesthesia, 55, 58, 77, 93, 114n10
synthesizer, synthesizing, 12, 36, 53, 65
Szymanowski, Karol, 76

Takemitsu, Toru, 18, 77
Tallinn, Estonia, 59
Tamine, Joëlle Gardes, 117n38
Tanglewood festival, 17
Tanner, Alain, 19, 29
tape music, tape material, 14, 15, 27, 30, 32, 34, 65, 70, 88
Tarkovsky, Andrei, 59, 85
Tarkovsky, Arseniy, 85
techniques. *See* playing techniques
tempo, 63, 78, 80
temporality. *See* time
texture, 32, 33, 37, 39, 43, 45, 46, 48, 49, 56, 66, 67, 77, 88, 90, 92, 99–100
Théâtre du Châtelet, 22, 46
Thibon, Gustave, 199n20
Thomas, Gavin, 112n17
timbre, 11, 12, 14, 16, 27, 32, 39, 47, 50, 53, 66, 67, 74, 75, 77, 88
time, 18, 33, 38, 54, 69, 74, 88
Tommassini, Anthony, 46, 113n47, 113n48
tonal music, tonality, 7, 8, 10, 38, 50, 73, 75, 78, 88
transformation (musical), 35, 36, 59
transition (musical), 27, 30, 32, 33, 38, 58, 66, 83–84, 92, 106

Uimola, Tanja, 116n13
Ülhermann, Jörg von, 50, 113n66
United States of America, 18, 22, 24, 47
University of California, San Diego, 107
Upshaw, Dawn, vii, 21, 111n55

Vandenheeden, Jan, 110n32
Varèse, Edgard, 115n29
Vaughan, Henry, 32
Viljanen, Taina. *See* Riikonen (née Viljanen), Taina
visual arts, 4, 58, 59–60, 74; drawing, 3, 4, 61–62; graphics, 5; paintings, 5
Vittes, Laurence, 112n23
Vivier, Claude, 11
vocal music, 6, 26, 27, 29, 40–42, 43–44, 46, 77, 85, 86–87, 93. *See also* opera
voice, 6, 12, 40, 41, 42, 43, 45, 48, 58, 64, 66, 70, 78, 80, 83, 86–87, 104

Wagner, Richard, 6, 100
Weil, Simone, 24, 50, 103–6, 107, 119n21, 119n23, 119n29, 119n33
Westdeutscher Rundfunk, 18
Wien Modern Festival, 18
woman composer, vii, 14, 16, 17, 28
womanhood, vii, 8, 16, 29, 33, 40–41, 46, 48, 95, 97, 101
Woolf, Virginia, 5

Xenakis, Iannis, 76

Young Nordic Music Festival, 8

Zimmermann, Bernd Alois, 5

PIRKKO MOISALA is a professor of musicology at the University of Helsinki, Finland. She is the coeditor of *Music and Gender* and is on the editorial board of the journal *Women and Music*.

WOMEN

COMPOSERS

Kaija Saariaho

Pirkko Moisala

The University of Illinois Press
is a founding member of the
Association of American University Presses.

Composed in 9.5/13 Janson
with Meta display
by Jim Proefrock
at the University of Illinois Press
Designed by Copenhaver Cumpston
Manufactured by Sheridan Books, Inc.

University of Illinois Press
1325 South Oak Street
Champaign, IL 61820-6903
www.press.uillinois.edu